100

THINGS TO DO IN
MILWAUKEE
BEFORE YOU
DIE

100
THINGS TO DO IN
MILWAUKEE
BEFORE YOU
DIE

• •

JENNIFER POSH

REEDY PRESS

Library of Congress Control Number: 2015942712

ISBN: 9781681060088

Design by Jill Halpin

Printed in the United States of America
15 16 17 18 19   5 4 3 2 1

Please note that websites, phone numbers, addresses, and company names are
subject to change or cancellation. We did our best to relay the most accurate
information available, but due to circumstances beyond our control, please do not
hold us liable for misinformation. When exploring new destinations, please do your
homework before you go.

CONTENTS

xi • Preface

xiii • Acknowledgments

1 • **Food and Drink**

2 • Take a Brewery Tour

4 • Try the Flavor of the Day at Kopp's Frozen Custard

5 • Dig into Friday Fish Fry

6 • Sip a Drink at Milwaukee's Oldest Cocktail Lounge

8 • Complete a Mission at the Safe House

10 • Try a Giant Pretzel

11 • Grab Lunch at the Milwaukee Public Market

12 • Munch on Some Cheese Curds

13 • Raise a Glass in a Beer Garden

14 • Get a Local Cup of Joe

16 • Taste Locally Made Liquor

18 • Take a Food Tour

19 • Tea at the Pfister

20 • Cooking Class (or Dinner) at Braise

21 • Get Spooked at a Haunted Bar

22   •   Sample Small Plates

24   •   Sip an Extreme Bloody Mary

25   •   Get Tropical at Tiki Bars

26   •   Explore Extensive Beer Lists in Bay View

28   •   Relax on Milwaukee's Best Patio

29   •   Treat Yourself to a Tasting Menu at Sanford

30   •   Sample the Freshest Cheese in the City

32   •   Geek Out at 42 Lounge

33   •   Close Wolski's

34   •   Play Some Ping-Pong

35   **Music and Entertainment**

36   •   Rock Out at the World's Largest Music Festival

38   •   See a Show at the Pabst Theater

39   •   Celebrate at Ethnic Festivals

40   •   Jam at Summer Concerts

42   •   Take Your Picture with the Bronze Fonz

43   •   See a Movie at the Oriental Theatre

44   •   Eat a Cream Puff at the State Fair

46   •   Walk on the Wild Side

47   •   Learn about an American Icon

48   •   A Night at the Theater

49 • See Broadway in Milwaukee

50 • Take in an Outdoor Movie for Grown-ups

51 • Get Lucky at the Casino

52 • Crack Up at the Longest Running Comedy Show

53 • Let Kids Explore a Pint-Sized Community

54 • Hit the Dance Floor at Mad Planet

55 • Introduce the Kids to Theater

56 • Vive la France!

57 • Watch the Jets at the Air Show

58 • Enjoy Sweet Strings at the Symphony

59 • Bask in the Ballet

61 **Sports and Recreation**

62 • Kayak through the City

63 • Catch a Game at Miller Park

64 • Explore the Oak Leaf Trail

65 • Cheer on the Bucks

66 • Play Beach Volleyball on Bradford Beach

68 • Go Sailing on Lake Michigan

69 • Explore Milwaukee's Free Outdoor Art Gallery

70 • Root for Roller Derby

71 • Explore the City on Two Wheels

72 • Bowl at Holler House

74 • Relax on a River Cruise

75 • Go on a Pedaling Pub Crawl

76 • Go Fly a Kite

77 • Check out a 24-Hour Bike Race

78 • Explore the Urban Outdoors

79 • Go Ice Skating Downtown

80 • Cheer on Rowing Teams on the Milwaukee River

81 • Be a Packer Backer

82 • Do the Wave for the Wave

83 • Meet the Raptors

84 • Watch the Ads Take the Ice

85 • **Culture and History**

86 • Visit the World's Sexiest Building

88 • Discover Discovery World

89 • Visit the Streets of Old Milwaukee

90 • See How the Beer Barons Lived

91 • Experience Art in Nature

92 • Travel the Horticultural World

93 • Celebrate Art on Gallery Night

94 • Step behind the Scenes at Historic Buildings

95 • Pay Your Respects to Milwaukee's Late Greats

96 • Tour the Basilica

97 • Walk through Milwaukee's History

98 • Visit a Medieval Church

99 • Explore the Original Soldiers Home

100 • Explore the Hidden Gems of the Museum Scene

102 • Tour Central Library

103 • See All the Best on a City Tour

104 • Get to Work at the Grohmann

105 • Take in Beautiful Homes in North Point

106 • Learn about Urban Farming

107 • Find Milwaukee Murals

109 • **Shopping and Fashion**

110 • Find Arts and Style in the Historic Third Ward

111 • Pick out a Dashing Hat

112 • Get Lost in Antiques on Second

113 • Stroll Through Charming Cedarburg

114 • Find German Heritage on Old World Third Street

116 • Shop Local at Sparrow Collective

117 • Shop for Italian Favorites

118 • Take Home Some Beer Memorabilia

119 • Get Hip at Indie Craft Fairs

120	•	Find What You Didn't Know You Were Looking For
121	•	Support Local Farmers All Year
122	•	Wander in Wauwatosa
124	•	Browse the Books at Boswell

125 • **Suggested Itineraries**

130 • **Events by Season**

132 • **Index**

• •

PREFACE

Milwaukee is, in my opinion, the best kept secret of the Midwest. It has all of the amenities of a big city—the award-winning chefs and acclaimed dining, world class arts and theater, professional sports teams, and exciting events—combined with the easy-going hospitality and charm of a small town. Yes, the locals really are as friendly as they say!

I've been in love with Milwaukee since I was a kid, riding the school bus downtown on a field trip to a museum and driving home at night after a festival, entranced by the city lights. I'm excited to have it as my home as an adult, and my favorite thing is to show friends who have never visited before all the parts of the city I love the most. With this book in your hand, I'm going to do the same for you!

This guidebook gives you a cross section of the city, from the must-sees to the quirky local secrets. Whether it's your first time in the city or you're a Milwaukeean looking to get to know it a little better, I hope that this book will inspire you to get out and explore Milwaukee.

• •

ACKNOWLEDGMENTS

First of all, the biggest thanks has to go to Milwaukee itself. Thank you for being the fun, creative, authentic, vibrant city that I'm proud to call home. This book wouldn't be possible without all of the great people, places, and businesses that make Milwaukee what it is!

Thank you to my family (my parents John and Sue and my sister Julie) for always supporting my writing. Thank you Megan for believing in my work and allowing me to pursue this opportunity. Big thanks go to Kaitlin and Misha for all their support during the writing process . . . I couldn't have done it without your advice and handholding! Everyone who listened to me freak out about deadlines and helped me whittle down my list: you know who are, and I salute you.

100

THINGS TO DO IN
MILWAUKEE
BEFORE YOU
DIE

FOOD
AND DRINK

TAKE A BREWERY TOUR

There's a reason Milwaukee is known as "Brew City." Brewing is one of the industries that the city was built on, and it's beer that "made Milwaukee famous." The city is full of beer history, but it's also the home of both macro and micro brewers, so don't miss the opportunity to see how those brews are made. At MillerCoors, you'll get a (free!) look at the production lines of one of the industry's giants, including a trip down to the caves where Frederick Miller used to cool his brews. Lakefront Brewery's hilarious tour is a great way to get to know the innovative microbrews that are currently produced in the city. Got the kids with you? Don't worry . . . Sprecher Brewing Company also brews delicious gourmet sodas, so the whole family can have a taste!

TIP

After the tour at Lakefront Brewery, you'll receive a coupon to enjoy a free Lakefront beer at many popular local establishments later that day. Make sure to save room in your schedule!

BE SURE TO VISIT

MillerCoors
4251 West State St.
Milwaukee, WI 53208
millercoors.com

Lake Front Brewery
1872 North Commerce St.
Milwaukee, WI 53212
lakefrontbrewery.com

Sprecher Brewing Company
701 W Glendale Ave.
Glendale, WI 53209
sprecherbrewery.com

TRY THE FLAVOR OF THE DAY
AT KOPP'S FROZEN CUSTARD

A richer and creamier version of ice cream, frozen custard is the cold dessert of choice for locals. There are lots of local spots to find this sweet treat, but Kopp's is a landmark for good reason. Kopp's has been serving up frozen custard and jumbo burgers since 1950 and is still going strong, with three locations in the Metro Milwaukee area today. The chocolate and vanilla custards are tried-and-true delicious, but the best part of going to Kopp's is trying one of their flavors of the day. The flavors range from classics like cookies 'n' cream and red raspberry to exotic treats like cherry amaretto cheesecake and German chocolate cake. Not indulgent enough for you? Try the sundae of the month instead!

Family friendly

Kopp's Frozen Custard
7631 W Layton Ave., Greenfield, WI 53220
kopps.com

DIG INTO
FRIDAY FISH FRY

One of Milwaukee's most distinctive traditions is the Friday fish fry. Born out of the need for non-meat options for the city's strong Catholic community, the fish fry is now a tradition embraced by all. It would be easier to list the restaurants that *don't* offer a fish fry on Friday than the ones that do, but there are some standout local spots. The Packing House has been repeatedly voted by locals as the best in Milwaukee and even offers a drive-up window for those who want their fish fry on the run. (Note: the drive-up window is cash only.) For the best atmosphere, stop at Lakefront Brewery Beer Hall. Each fish fry is accompanied by a performance from the Brewhaus Polka Kings.

Family friendly

The Packing House
900 E Layton Ave., Milwaukee, WI 53207
packinghousemke.com

Lakefront Brewery
1872 North Commerce St., Milwaukee, WI 53212
lakefrontbrewery.com

SIP A DRINK
AT MILWAUKEE'S OLDEST COCKTAIL LOUNGE

The bartenders at Bryant's Cocktail Lounge can mix over five hundred different cocktails, but you won't find a menu on the premises. Instead, the staff will guide you to your perfect cocktail based on your own preferences. Order by spirit, flavor, strength, color, and more. Founded in 1938, Bryant's is especially famous for their Depression-era cocktails. The founder, Bryant Sharp, is credited with the invention of the Pink Squirrel and the Banshee.

Honored as a semifinalist for "Best Bar Program" by the James Beard Awards, Bryant's is a true local gem. It's dark and intimate inside, taking you back in time to the classic days of the swanky cocktail lounge. It's a great spot to snuggle up with a sweetie, but it's also a ton of fun to take a big group—and taste everyone's drink!

Bryant's Cocktail Lounge
1579 S 9th St., Milwaukee, WI 53204
bryantscocktaillounge.com

TIP

If you come during winter,
ask for the Christmas punch.

COMPLETE A MISSION
AT THE SAFE HOUSE

Live out your James Bond fantasy at Milwaukee's most secret bar. An unassuming door marked "International Exports Ltd." is your portal into the world of espionage. Miss Moneypenny will ask you for the password, but don't worry if you don't know it . . . she'll give you some other task to prove your loyalty, and then you're in. Once inside, enjoy martinis that are shaken (not stirred) by flying through pneumatic tubes, a full menu, and, of course, tons of kitschy spy memorabilia. Make sure to take the time to poke around in every nook and cranny . . . you never know what you might find! When it's time to go, you might even be able to use your newly honed espionage skills to find the secret exit.

Family friendly until 8 p.m.

Safe House
779 North Front St., Milwaukee, WI 53202
safe-house.com

TIP

If you're celebrating a special occasion, contact Control before you arrive to arrange for a "Hail to the Chief" for a gentleman agent or an "On Her Majesty's Secret Service" for a femme fatale.

TRY
A GIANT PRETZEL

Milwaukee's strong German heritage is still an important part of the city's identity, and the best way to explore a cultural legacy is (of course) to taste it! Open since 1902, Mader's was originally more of a bar than a restaurant, but Prohibition swayed Charles Mader to focus on his kitchen. Over a century later, we should all be grateful he did. Through the years, the city's premiere German restaurant has played host to celebrities from John F. Kennedy to Katy Perry. Voted the most famous German restaurant in America, at Mader's you'll be able to admire a $3 million collection of art, suits of medieval armor, and antiques while you dine on classic German dishes such as sauerbraten, wiener schnitzel and rouladen. Don't miss their famous giant pretzel!

Family friendly

Mader's
1041 N Old World Third St., Milwaukee, WI 53203
madersrestaurant.com

GRAB LUNCH
AT THE MILWAUKEE PUBLIC MARKET

There's only one place you can find sandwiches, sushi, Mexican, Middle Eastern, pastries, and wine all under one roof. The Milwaukee Public Market has been ranked one of the best public markets in the country. With around twenty unique local vendors, it's the perfect place to stop for lunch or to pick up some snacks or souvenirs to take home. Try the famous lobster dinner special at St. Paul Fish Company, with hand-dipped chocolates from Kehr's Candies for dessert, and a glass of wine from Thief Wine Bar to wash it all down. For an ultimate Milwaukee souvenir, purchase some spice mixes from The Spice House. Many of the mixes are named after famous Milwaukee neighborhoods. The second floor is full of tables where you can sit and enjoy your purchases while you watch the bustle of the market below.

Milwaukee Public Market
400 N Water St., Milwaukee, WI 53202
milwaukeepublicmarket.com

MUNCH
ON SOME CHEESE CURDS

A fresh cheese curd is famous for its trademark squeak between the teeth, but the curds you'll find on the menu at local watering holes won't squeal. Deep-fried cheese curds are a beloved Milwaukee appetizer and you won't want to leave town without trying a greasy basket full (with ranch and/or marinara for dipping). Any pub worth its salt will have them on the menu, so don't worry about picking a restaurant just for its curds. But if you're in the market, some of the best in the city can be found at Jackson's Blue Ribbon Pub. When you eat here, you add a side of history to your side dish because you will find this pub inside the Brewhouse Inn & Suites in the renovated Pabst Brewery Complex.

Family friendly

Jackson's Blue Ribbon Pub
1203 N 10th St., Milwaukee, WI 53205
jacksonsbrp.com

RAISE A GLASS
IN A BEER GARDEN

Throughout the summer and early fall, beer gardens spring forth in Milwaukee's parks and green spaces, creating friendly communal gathering spaces. Many vendors will sell concessions such as hot dogs, bratwursts, and traditional German pretzels, but you're welcome to bring your own picnic if you so choose. One of the most popular spots is the Estabrook Beer Garden in Estabrook Park, open Thursday through Sunday. Modeled after the *biergartens* of modern-day Munich, this is the first truly public beer garden in America since Prohibition. Get your beer in the traditional liter or half-liter heavy glass mug (deposit required) or bring your own favorite stein. The beer garden is set along the banks of the Milwaukee River, accessible by major bike trails. Guests arrive at this convenient location by kayak, canoe, automobile, bicycle, or foot. Estabrook Park also features disc golf, playgrounds, soccer fields, a dog park, and more.

Family friendly

Estabrook Beer Garden
4600 Estabrook Drive, Milwaukee, WI 53217
oldgermanbeerhall.com/estabrook-beer-garden

GET A LOCAL
CUP OF JOE

Beer isn't the only thing brewing in Milwaukee. The city is also passionately devoted to coffee and a number of local roasters and cafes serve this delightful beverage. Colectivo Coffee and Stone Creek Coffee lead the pack in locations, with twelve and ten cafes in the Milwaukee area, respectively, but Anodyne Coffee's two cafes are both popular with locals. Anodyne recently added a wood-fired pizza oven to their Bay View cafe, providing yet another reason to check it out. You can visit two Colectivo locations to take a look at the behind-the-scenes preparation. Coffee enthusiasts, you can stop by the cafe attached to their Riverwest roastery to see where every bean is roasted by hand. If you are more interested in carbs than caffeine, visit the Bay View location, where the staff bakes fresh breads and pastries to distribute to all locations. Skip the Starbucks while you're in town.

Family friendly

THE BEST COFFEE IN TOWN

Colectivo Coffee
Various locations
colectivocoffee.com

Stone Creek Coffee
Various locations
stonecreekcoffee.com

Anodyne Coffee
Various locations
anodynecoffee.com

TASTE
LOCALLY MADE LIQUOR

It's no surprise that Milwaukee is home to great craft breweries, but fans of local libations can't miss out on the local craft distilleries. The first distillery in Wisconsin since Prohibition is Great Lakes Distillery, a small-batch distillery creating award-winning liquors through old-world methods. If you take a tour of the facility, you will enjoy a tasting flight of six of their spirits, from whiskey to absinthe. If you just drop in, you can still enjoy a delicious, locally crafted cocktail at the bar. Another local distillery is Central Standard Craft Distillery, which serves up vodka, gin, and white whiskey both behind the bar and during tours and tastings. Plus, Central Standard is located right next door to Milwaukee Brewing Company, which is perfect if you're looking to explore both brewing and distilling in one easy trip.

Great Lakes Distillery
616 W Virginia St., Milwaukee, WI 53204
greatlakesdistillery.com

Central Standard Craft Distillery
613 S 2nd St., Milwaukee, WI 53204
thecentralstandard.com

TIP

Make sure to keep an eye out
for local bottles behind the bar
when you're out on the town for
a true local experience.

TAKE
A FOOD TOUR

It's always hard to find a way to fit all the fantastic restaurants you want to try into your visit, especially when you're only in town for a few days. Knock out some of the best in Milwaukee in one fell swoop on Milwaukee Food & City Tours. Take a walking tour through popular neighborhoods to experience their historic past and bustling present. You may enjoy tasting the Italian heritage of Brady Street or checking out the best "Bloodies & Beers" of hip Bay View. Alternatively, try a themed bus tour, where you might taste classic Milwaukee pizzas or explore historic bars that date back to pre-Prohibition. No matter which tour you choose to take, you'll get a meal's worth of samples from each stop and a hearty helping of local knowledge to wash it down.

Family friendly (some tours 21+)

Milwaukee Food & City Tours
Various locations
milwaukeefoodtours.com

TEA
AT THE PFISTER

The Pfister Hotel, an elegant Milwaukee landmark that was inspired by the grand hotels of Europe, still maintains its Victorian-era decor. Built in 1893, the Pfister has been a symbol of elegance in Milwaukee and throughout the Midwest for well over a century. Become a part of its luxurious history and take a respite from the busy modern world with an afternoon tea service. Using an all-silver service, including a replica of an eighteenth–century self-tipping teapot, the Tea Butler will attend to you. You can't fail to enjoy the afternoon as you sip your tea and nibble on treats such as chocolate-covered strawberries, fresh scones, and curried quail eggs. Tea is held on the twenty-third floor of the hotel, treating you to a panoramic view of downtown Milwaukee and Lake Michigan. Reservations are required.

Pfister Hotel
424 East Wisconsin Ave., Milwaukee, WI 53202
thepfisterhotel.com

COOKING CLASS
(OR DINNER) AT BRAISE

Braise is the city's only community-supported restaurant. In addition to the hyperlocal, super-seasonal menu they serve in the restaurant, Braise also runs a culinary school and a restaurant–supported agriculture program. This program makes it easier for other restaurants in the area to obtain local, sustainable food. Definitely stop in for dinner (chef/owner Dave Swanson has been repeatedly recognized by the James Beard Association), but if you're a true foodie take it to the next level with a cooking class. Let the expert chefs at Braise teach you everything from how to whip up the basics of Mexican street food to how to bake great breakfast pastries. You'll get to take the fruits of your labor home, but (even better) you'll be able to keep your new skills forever!

Braise Restaurant
1101 S 2nd St., Milwaukee, WI 53204
braiselocalfood.com

GET SPOOKED
AT A HAUNTED BAR

There are two reasons to visit Shaker's Cigar Bar: either you want cigars and classic vintage cocktails or you want a good haunting. Yes, it's true: this bar is haunted! Originally built in 1894, Shaker's became a distribution center for Schlitz Brewery before spending many years as a speakeasy. Today, it's best known as the residence of several "entities." You can take a guided tour through the many floors of Shaker's to learn more about the ghosts that dwell there. Or, if you're of particularly hardy stock, you can even spend the night in the haunted penthouse. Not in the mood for otherworldly spirits? Just stop by to enjoy a cigar alongside a cocktail (absinthe, perhaps?) and soak in the atmosphere.

Shaker's Cigar Bar
422 S 2nd St., Milwaukee, WI 53204
shakerscigarbar.com

SAMPLE
SMALL PLATES

If you're the type who can't help but take a nibble off of everyone else's plate at dinner, you won't want to miss Milwaukee's vibrant small plates and tapas scene. From international flair to regional favorites (like a cheese plate . . . it is Wisconsin after all!), these restaurants let you try it all. Order a few for the table and don't be shy about fighting over the last bite of that favorite dish. There's no shame in that! Try these local hotspots to get your small plates fix.

WHERE TO FIND TAPAS

La Merenda
125 East National Ave.
Milwaukee, WI 53204
lamerenda125.com

Wolf Peach
1818 N Hubbard St.
Milwaukee, WI 53212
wolf-peach.com

Odd Duck
2352 S Kinnickinnic Ave.
Milwaukee, WI 53207
oddduckrestaurant.com

Balzac
1716 N Arlington Place
Milwaukee, WI 53202
balzacwinebar.com

SIP
AN EXTREME BLOODY MARY

This is a brunch-loving town, so it's no surprise that locals love a good Bloody Mary. Garnishes in Milwaukee go far beyond the limp stick of celery you may be picturing. Our Bloody Marys are topped with anything and everything you can imagine, from bacon-wrapped shrimp and tiny cheeseburgers to sausage sticks and giant pickles. Some of them are practically a meal themselves! The title of Best Bloody in Milwaukee is hotly contested, and it's hard to go wrong with a house specialty. But if you're a true devotee of over-the-top brunch beverages, don't miss out on those served at Sobelman's Pub-n-Grill. Their "Chicken-Fried Bloody Beast" is a Bloody Mary pitcher that comes topped with, yes, an entire fried chicken. You'll probably need a few friends to help you out with that one.

Sobelman's Pub-n-Grill
1900 W St. Paul Ave., Milwaukee, WI 53233
milwaukeesbestburgers.com

GET TROPICAL
AT TIKI BARS

Sometimes you need some tropical inspiration to get through a cold winter, so it should come as no surprise that Milwaukee is home to two tiki bars. The classic choice, Foundation Tiki Bar, is a dark and mysterious slice of paradise, bursting with intriguing tiki artifacts. The newcomer, Lucky Joe's Tiki Room, has a bit more modern kitsch to it, with color-changing tiki god statues and great nightly specials. Both supply tantalizing drinks from the tropics (with a whole lot of rum), many of which are available in a collectible mug to take home. Collectors beware: Lucky Joe's also offers a collectible mug of the month in addition to their standard supply. If you're up for an island adventure even though you're by the shore of the Great Lakes and not the South Seas, there's no reason not to visit both while you're in town.

Foundation Tiki Bar
2718 N Bremen St., Milwaukee, WI 53212
foundationbar.com

Lucky Joe's Tiki Room
196 S 2nd St., Milwaukee, WI 53204
luckyjoestiki.com

EXPLORE
EXTENSIVE BEER LISTS
IN BAY VIEW

If you're looking for the widest selection of brews (and why wouldn't you be?), you're most likely to find it in Bay View, an eclectic neighborhood on Milwaukee's south side. All three of the Milwaukee bars named to *Draft Magazine*'s 100 Best Beer Bars in America list are located in this neighborhood. In Bay View, you will also find several local favorites. Their beer lists are so extensive that you just might find yourself with an entire book handed to you, but don't worry—these bartenders love to make suggestions!

FIVE TOP OPTIONS
FOR BAY VIEW BREWS

Sugar Maple
441 E Lincoln Ave.
Milwaukee, WI 53207
mysugarmaple.com

Romans' Pub
3475 S Kinnickinnic Ave.
Milwaukee, WI 53207
romanspub.com

Palm Tavern
2989 S Kinnickinnic Ave.
Milwaukee, WI 53207
twitter.com/palmtavern

Burnhearts
2599 S Logan Ave.
Milwaukee, WI 53207
burnhearts.tumblr.com

Cafe Centraal
2306 S Kinnickinnic Ave.
Milwaukee, WI 53207
cafecentraal.com

RELAX
ON MILWAUKEE'S BEST PATIO

One of Milwaukee's best patios is also one of its best-kept secrets. More easily accessible by boat than by car, you'll probably suspect you took a wrong turn somewhere on your way to Barnacle Bud's. It's tucked away on the river in an industrial area, so you'll drive over gravel and past more than one loading dock. But if you persevere, you'll be rewarded with a relaxing visit to a beach-style shack; locals flock to its patio in the summer months. Check out the oyster bar and order up some Bloody Marys for an excellent afternoon. If you have your boat with you (or rented one somewhere up the river), feel free to cruise up to one of the slips for a true riverfront experience.

Barnacle Bud's
1955 S Hilbert St., Milwaukee, WI 53207
barnacle-buds.com

TREAT YOURSELF
TO A TASTING MENU AT SANFORD

Sandy D'Amato, an icon of the local culinary scene, was the first Milwaukee chef to be named the James Beard Award's Best Chef: Midwest (1996). In 1989, he founded Sanford Restaurant, which quickly became one of the most renowned restaurants in the Midwest, serving creative, upscale New American cuisine. In 2012, Sandy sold the restaurant to his longtime chef de cuisine, Justin Aprahamian, who promptly won his own title as Best Chef: Midwest (2014). This restaurant with a pedigree more than lives up to its titles. You can't go wrong ordering from their menu, but if you truly want the ultimate Milwaukee culinary experience, go for the Seven-Course Surprise Tasting Menu. Let the chef guide you through a custom menu on a journey of taste sensations.

Sanford Restaurant
1547 N Jackson St., Milwaukee, WI 53202
sanfordrestaurant.com

SAMPLE
THE FRESHEST CHEESE IN THE CITY

You have to make time for cheese while you're in the dairy state! Clock Shadow Creamery in the Walker's Point neighborhood is Wisconsin's only urban cheese factory. They make traditional Wisconsin cheese curds, cheddar, quark, ricotta, chévre, queso blanco, and more. This neighborhood is quickly becoming a haven for innovative and artisan food. You can take an educational and delicious tour of the factory to learn more about the history of cheese making. You'll get the answer to burning questions such as, "What makes cheese curds squeak?" Of course, you'll also have the chance to sample some freshly made Milwaukee cheese! Fresh cheese curds are made every Wednesday and Friday, so go then if you want to taste the freshest of the fresh. Don't forget to pick up a few of your favorites to take home after the tour in their factory store.

Family friendly

Clock Shadow Creamery
138 W Bruce St., Milwaukee, WI 53204

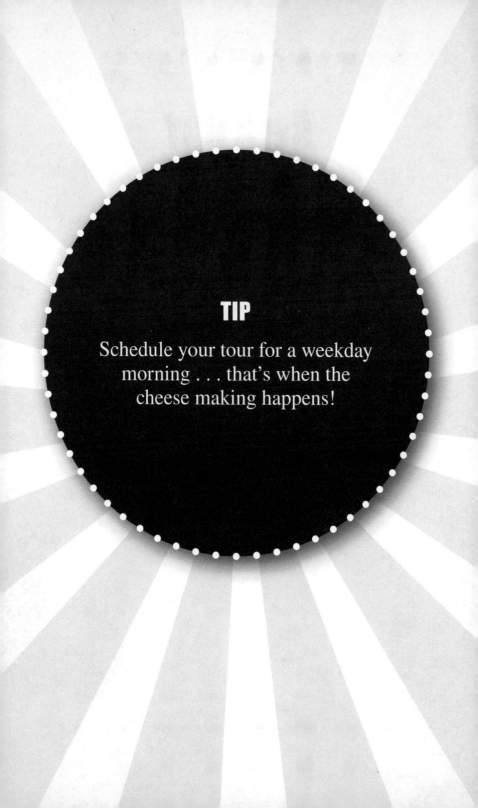

TIP

Schedule your tour for a weekday morning . . . that's when the cheese making happens!

GEEK OUT
AT 42 LOUNGE

Have you ever been to a nightclub for nerds? Simply take out the TV showing the football game and add *Doctor Who*, cosplay parties, and consoles for gaming. This is the atmosphere of 42 Lounge, Milwaukee's swanky nightlife home for all things geek. All of the games are free to play, so come hang out and have a good time. In addition to its impressive selection of beer, wine, and mead, 42 Lounge is famous for its geeky themed cocktails. Sip on an adult beverage named after one of your favorite characters or try a drink whose namesake was made famous by pop culture. You don't have to be a gamer to enjoy this classy downtown lounge.

42 Lounge
326 E Mason St., Milwaukee, WI 53202
42lounge.com

CLOSE WOLSKI'S

Family owned for more than one hundred years, Wolski's Tavern is the quintessential Milwaukee neighborhood bar. Offering free popcorn and free steel-tipped darts to go along with your libations, it's an iconic local watering hole that's a great place to hang out for a night. The thing that really makes Wolski's famous, though, is its bumper stickers. Since the 1970s, Wolski's has been rewarding customers who stick it out until closing time with an "I Closed Wolski's" sticker. Now these stickers have traveled all around the world and have been spotted everywhere from Paris to Japan; they also appear (unsurprisingly) on many a Midwesterner's bumper. Closing Wolski's is a rite of passage for locals and visitors alike, so get ready for a late night!

Wolski's Tavern
1836 N Pulaski St., Milwaukee, WI 53202
wolskis.com

PLAY SOME PING-PONG

It's true: you can play ping-pong and enjoy lunch (or a few drinks) at the same time. Evolution Gastro Pong (known to locals as "Evo") is a trendy, high-energy bar and restaurant with thirteen table-tennis courts on cushioned Olympic-competition flooring just waiting for you to pick up a paddle and play. In addition to providing pool, darts, and giant Jenga, Evolution offers two bars, a pro shop, private rooms, and a full-service restaurant. Bring the family for some indoor fun during the day, or get together with your friends to enjoy an adult beverage and active entertainment in the evening. Whether you're a table tennis enthusiast or an occasional basement player, this unique bar is a cool and stylish spot that's fun for all ages.

Family friendly

Evolution Gastro Pong
233 E Chicago St., Milwaukee, WI 53202
evolutionmke.com

MUSIC AND ENTERTAINMENT

ROCK OUT
AT THE WORLD'S LARGEST MUSIC FESTIVAL

Summerfest is the iconic Milwaukee summer experience. It's the largest music festival in the world and it takes place right on the scenic shores of Lake Michigan. Over eight hundred bands perform over the course of eleven days. Expect to see both major arena tours and local cover bands rocking out on the eleven stages. Almost every genre is represented, so you're sure to find something that you like, be it pop, country, alternative, rock, or reggae. The seventy-five-acre festival grounds are permanent, which means you don't have to deal with mud, portable toilets, or outdoor sleeping arrangements . . . at this festival, you can enjoy the music and the comforts of a nice hotel. Stroll the grounds to shop for everything from clothes to jewelry to music-themed memorabilia, purchase food from local vendors, and participate in interactive exhibits. Both the dedicated kids' stage featuring magicians, dancing, puppets, and more and the large playground make this event a popular stop for families.

Henry Maier Festival Park
200 N Harbor Dr., Milwaukee, WI 53202
summerfest.com

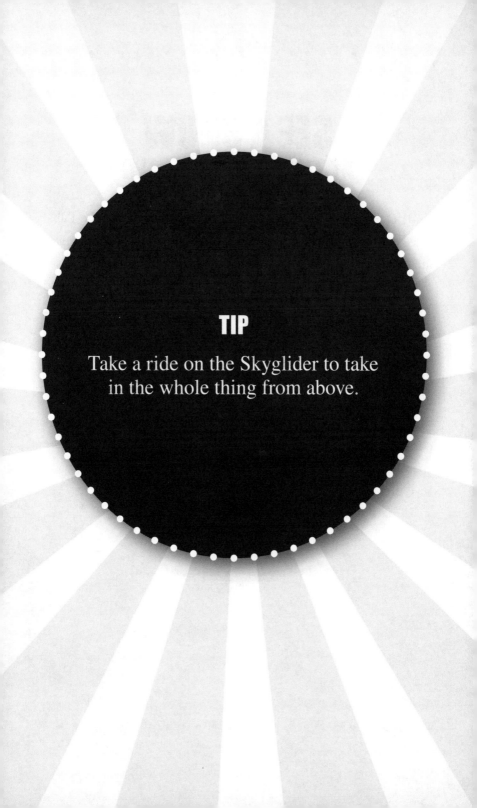

TIP

Take a ride on the Skyglider to take in the whole thing from above.

SEE A SHOW
AT THE PABST THEATER

Built in 1895 by beer baron Captain Frederick Pabst, the Pabst Theater is known as "Milwaukee's jewel box." The opulent theater was built in the baroque style of the great opera houses of Europe. It features a stunning Austrian crystal chandelier and a staircase of white Italian Carrara marble. A proscenium arch, detailed in gold leaf, frames the stage. Although the Pabst is the fourth-oldest continually operating theater in the United States, it offers entirely modern entertainment. Over two hundred acts, from star comedians to great bands, appear at the Pabst every year. The theater is famous for the five-star treatment it gives performers and a number of popular acts come to Milwaukee specifically to perform at the Pabst. Come see what makes them love this historic venue!

Family friendly, depending on event

Pabst Theater
144 East Wells St., Milwaukee, WI 53202
pabsttheater.org

CELEBRATE
AT ETHNIC FESTIVALS

Milwaukee is known as the "City of Festivals," and you'll find a different one going on almost every weekend in the summer. Celebrate Milwaukee's diverse population with food, music, dance, history, and more at the permanent lakefront festival grounds. Many of these festivals are the largest cultural heritage celebrations of their kind in the world. They bring together people from all over the globe to experience history and heritage in a fun and vibrant way. Dance the polka and nosh on spanferkel at German Fest, try some pierogi at Polish Fest, watch hurling and currach races at Irish Fest, explore traditional arts and crafts at Mexican Fiesta, and more. These festivals are a great way to celebrate your own heritage or experience an entirely new culture.

Family friendly

Henry Maier Festival Park
200 North Harbor Drive, Milwaukee, WI 53202
milwaukeeworldfestival.com/calendar-of-events

JAM
AT SUMMER CONCERTS

There's a free outdoor concert series on almost every night of the week during the summer in Milwaukee. These concert series are full-on events that bring together music groups, vendors, and entire communities to celebrate the summer. Whether you prefer popular cover bands or classical ensembles, you're sure to find a series that's right for you. Get dinner from a food truck or a local vendor and enjoy a picnic in the park while the band plays. With a diverse assortment of performers from around town and across the country, there's always something new to enjoy. A few favorites include Chill on the Hill in Humboldt Park on Tuesdays, River Rhythms in the riverside Pere Marquette Park on Wednesdays, and Jazz in the Park at Cathedral Square Park on Thursdays. A lot of local band shells and pavilions come to life in the summer, so you may catch some tunes simply by taking a stroll on a nice evening.

Family friendly

110 W Washington St., Milwaukee, WI 46204
www.rhythmdiscoverycenter.org

FAVORITE SUMMER CONCERTS

Chill on the HIll
Humboldt Park
3000 South Howell Ave.
Milwaukee, WI 53207
bayviewneighborhood.org/chill_on_the_hill

River Rhythms
900 N Plankinton Ave
Milwaukee, WI 53202
westown.org/neighborhood-events/river-rhythms-2

Jazz in the Park
825 North Jefferson St.
Milwaukee, WI 53202
easttown.com/events/jazz-in-the-park

TAKE YOUR PICTURE
WITH THE BRONZE FONZ

Without a doubt, the number one photo-op on the Milwaukee RiverWalk is the Bronze Fonz. The popular sitcom *Happy Days* was set in 1950s Milwaukee; local booster groups raised the funds to erect this statue of Arthur "The Fonz" Fonzarelli in his trademark "thumbs-up" pose. Stop and put your own thumbs up for a perfectly Milwaukee picture. A hearty "Ayyy!" isn't mandatory, but it sure is fun!

Family friendly

Bronze Fonz
Milwaukee RiverWalk, just south of Wells St.

SEE A MOVIE
AT THE ORIENTAL THEATRE

The Oriental Theatre, the only remaining great, glamorous "movie palace" of Milwaukee, originally opened in 1927. Most of the original design, featuring elegant East Indian–inspired mosaics and stunning elephants, remains to this day. The Kimball theatre pipe organ still introduces the 7 p.m. showing on Friday and Saturday nights, just like in the old days. Today, the theater screens both blockbusters and independent films on its three screens and serves as the home theater for the Milwaukee Film Festival each fall. The Oriental holds the world record for most continuous screenings of the cult classic, *The Rocky Horror Picture Show*. Stop by on the second Saturday of every month to see the movie with a live shadow cast.

Family friendly

Oriental Theatre
2230 N Farwell Ave., Milwaukee, WI 53202
landmarktheatres.com/milwaukee/oriental-theatre

EAT A CREAM PUFF
AT THE STATE FAIR

Held just outside the city, the Wisconsin State Fair is an eleven-day whirlwind of food, music, animals, and fun. Food on sticks (often deep-fried or dunked in chocolate) is the name of the game, but the truly iconic fair food is the cream puff. Sold since 1924, this is the most popular food item at the fair with an average of 350,000 served each year. Between your cream puffs, you can stop at the livestock barns, explore the Wisconsin Products Pavilion to see all of the great things made in state, enjoy demonstrations and shopping in the Expo Center, and, of course, ride the rides on the midway. There's live music across the grounds all day and headliner concerts on the historic Milwaukee Mile racetrack in the evenings.

Family friendly

Wisconsin State Fair Park
640 S 84th St., West Allis, WI 53214
wistatefair.com

TIP

The Department of Natural Resources's Natural Resources Park is an educational oasis celebrating the outdoors. Learn about fisheries, conservation, forestry, and more.

WALK
ON THE WILD SIDE

Open 365 days a year, the nationally recognized Milwaukee County Zoo is one of the most popular attractions in the area. Get in touch with your wild side by visiting the more than 2,500 animals, representing 300 species and housed in 200 acres of natural habitats. In addition to animals, the zoo has great activities for people of all ages. Educational shows like the Birds of Prey Show and Oceans of Fun Seal & Sea Lion Show bring the animals up close and personal. You can get even closer by feeding the giraffes and goats. Kids love to ride the train that circles the grounds, and the Sky Trail® Wisconsin Adventure Zone challenges all ages with a five-hundred-foot zip line, climbing wall, and ropes course.

Family friendly

Milwaukee County Zoo
10001 W Bluemound Rd., Milwaukee, WI 53226
milwaukeezoo.org

LEARN
ABOUT AN AMERICAN ICON

Take a walk on a different kind of wild side. The Harley-Davidson Motor Company was founded in Milwaukee in 1903 and, over a century later, still makes the city its home. Whether you're a devoted biker or just interested in learning more about an iconic American brand, stop in at the world's only Harley-Davidson Museum. The museum is full of informative and interactive exhibits. See the oldest known Harley in existence, Serial Number One, then celebrate custom culture with some of the most creative bikes ever built. There's an experience gallery full of Harley-Davidson bikes that you can try on for size; kids can try on pint-sized Harley gear and design their dream bikes. Dedicated Harley fans, don't miss the special tours through the museum that take you out to the Pilgrim Road Powertrain Operations facility and into the private Harley-Davidson archives.

Family friendly

Harley-Davidson Museum
400 W Canal St., Milwaukee, WI 53201
h-dmuseum.com

A NIGHT
AT THE THEATER

If you're a theater lover, take in a performance at the Milwaukee Repertory Theater, a Milwaukee classic. "The Rep," as locals call it, has been nationally recognized as one of the top regional theaters in the country for more than sixty years. This professional acting company puts on diverse shows each year, from modern dramas to beloved musicals. Built inside a converted power plant, the Rep's theater complex is home to three distinct performance spaces: the Stackner Cabaret, the Stiemke Studio, and the main stage, the Quadracci Powerhouse Theater. The Quadracci Powerhouse is a unique theater featuring a thrust stage that brings the actors close to the audience, making each performance feel intimate despite its size.

Milwaukee Rep
108 E Wells St., Milwaukee WI 53202
milwaukeerep.com

SEE BROADWAY
IN MILWAUKEE

Milwaukee's premiere performing arts venue, the Marcus Center for the Performing Arts, is as close as you can get to a one–stop shop to appreciate the arts in Milwaukee. If you're looking for a little razzle dazzle while you're in town, you'll find it here. The Marcus Center hosts touring productions of Broadway and Off-Broadway shows throughout the year, bringing the biggest and brightest shows to the city. The venue itself is also the brightest in town, glowing every night with a multicolored light show. You can't miss it! The Marcus Center is also the home of great local performing arts companies such as the Florentine Opera, the Milwaukee Symphony Orchestra, the Milwaukee Ballet, and the renowned First Stage Children's Theater.

Family friendly depending on show

Marcus Center for the Performing Arts
929 N Water St., Milwaukee, WI 53202
marcuscenter.org

TAKE IN
AN OUTDOOR MOVIE FOR GROWN-UPS

It's the drive-in without all that driving! Grab your blanket and camp chair, and head down to the shores of Lake Michigan to watch a movie with a few hundred of your closest friends. Fish Fry & a Flick is a free summer movie series for adults, which brings movie fans down to the lawn of Discovery World on select Friday nights throughout the summer. They get to watch a movie and have a good time participating in a classic Milwaukee past time: fish fry! Enjoy the delicious fish fry and other treats available for purchase throughout the evening (kids are welcome to attend during this portion of the event); once dusk comes, it's time for the (often R-rated) movie to begin. The series features both buzz-worthy hits and cult classics, offering a little something for every movie fan.

Fish Fry & a Flick
Discovery World
500 N Harbor Dr., Milwaukee, WI 53202
pointfishfryandaflick.com

GET LUCKY
AT THE CASINO

Do you feel lucky? Potawatomi Hotel & Casino, just minutes away from downtown, is the most popular entertainment destination in the state. There's plenty to keep your attention if you're the gaming type. Attractions include high-stakes bingo, nearly one hundred table games, twenty poker tables, almost three thousand slot machines, and an off-track betting room that keeps you in the heart of the action. Bar 360, located in the center of the gaming floor, is the perfect place to sit under a rainbow light show and watch all of the action. If you're not a gambler, don't worry! There are seven restaurants on-site (including the extremely popular Dream Dance Steak) as well as an intimate five-hundred-seat theater that hosts touring musicians, comedians, and more.

Potawatomi Hotel & Casino
1721 W Canal St., Milwaukee, WI 53233
paysbig.com

CRACK UP
AT THE LONGEST RUNNING COMEDY SHOW

This isn't comedy about sports; this is where improv comedy becomes a sport. ComedySportz is the longest running comedy show in town and has entertained audiences of all ages for over thirty years. The game has now spread to cities all over the world, but it started right here in Milwaukee. With a referee and two teams, the audience helps bring each match to life with suggestions that fuel the game. The audience's applause earns points for the comedians. Every ComedySportz show is appropriate for all ages. You can expect to see grandparents, college students, Girl Scouts, and everyone in between. If you loved "Whose Line Is It Anyway," you have to catch a match (ComedySportz predates "Whose Line" by four years!). There's a full bar and restaurant on-site, so make a night of it.

Family friendly

ComedySportz
420 S 1st St., Milwaukee, WI 53202
comedysportzmilwaukee.com

LET KIDS EXPLORE
A PINT-SIZED COMMUNITY

Designed especially for kids aged ten years and younger, Betty Brinn Children's Museum is an interactive museum that lets kids explore the world around them. "Home Town" is a kid-sized community where kids can visit a pretend motorcycle dealership, a post office, a grocery store, a TV studio, a construction site, a bank, and more. "Word Headquarters" is a pretend communications company that helps kids learn about the importance of literacy. A giant interactive board game lets them play their way to a healthy lifestyle. Children are also invited to "be a maker" and to tinker, create, and explore freely in a special space filled with tools and materials. Rotating special exhibits and seasonally open outdoor spaces round out this unique museum experience that every kid will love.

Family friendly

Betty Brinn Children's Museum
929 E Wisconsin Ave., Milwaukee, WI 53202
bbcmkids.org

HIT THE DANCE FLOOR
AT MAD PLANET

Come let loose at the city's hottest dance party. If you're picturing a slick club full of strobe lights with a DJ blaring the latest electro-hits, you're a little bit off. Keep colorful lights and a DJ, but add a little bit of funk (for example, decorative mannequin parts), and you've got Mad Planet. This alt-rock dance club is a popular venue for both local and touring bands as well as DJs hosting retro parties. Mad Planet is perhaps most famous for their throwback parties on Friday nights; the music takes you back to the 1980s and '90s for a retro dance party that can't be beat. Looking to go back another decade or two? This club also hosts the Get Down, an all-vinyl funk and soul jam fest on select Saturdays.

Mad Planet
533 E Center St., Milwaukee, WI 53212
mad-planet.net

INTRODUCE THE KIDS
TO THEATER

First Stage, one of the nation's most renowned children's theaters and the second-largest theater company in Milwaukee, is the perfect place for kids and adults to discover the joy of the arts together. First Stage produces shows with age-appropriate casting, so you'll be entertained by a company of talented youth actors alongside adult professionals. Every season, this theatre offers shows aimed toward a variety of age levels, from toddlers to teens, inspired by the world of children's literature. In addition to their traditional season of shows, First Stage presents the First Steps series, which introduces children between the ages of three and six years old to theater in a lively, engaging way. A select performance in the First Steps series is adapted to a sensory-friendly performance designed for children with autism and their families.

Family friendly

First Stage Children's Theater
Marcus Center for the Performing Arts
929 N Water St., Milwaukee, WI 53202
firststage.org

VIVE LA FRANCE!

Bastille Days, one of the nation's largest French-themed celebrations, happens right in the heart of downtown Milwaukee. Best of all, it's free! Each summer, a pint-sized Paris (including a forty-three-foot Eiffel Tower) springs up in Cathedral Square Park and the surrounding blocks. The celebration is complete with roaming street performers, an international marketplace, French cuisine, chef and wine demonstrations, can-can dancers, and more. Come and stroll through this vibrant street festival as chalk artists transform the sidewalks into works of art, vendors serve up French treats (for example, crepes), and merry participants sip champagne. If you're the athletic type, you can help kick off the festivities during the evening of the opening day at the annual 5k fun run/walk, "Storm the Bastille."

Family friendly

Bastille Days
Cathedral Square Park
520 E Wells St., Milwaukee, WI 53202
easttown.com/events/bastille-days

WATCH THE JETS
AT THE AIR SHOW

Summer brings the roar of jet engines to the city when the Milwaukee Air & Water Show takes to the lake and to the skies. Known as the "largest two-day event in Wisconsin," this show has been known to attract over one million people to the lakefront . . . now that's a block party! The show is free and can be enjoyed at parks and beaches all along Milwaukee's lakefront. Ticketed reserved seating is available at the center point of the show if you want the ultimate view of the action. Come watch both military and civilian teams perform their best tricks. Crowd favorites include precision aerobatics from jet teams and parachuting demonstrations. Bring along a picnic and have a beach day unlike any other.

Family friendly

Milwaukee Air & Water Show
Shores of Lake Michigan
milwaukeeairshow.com

ENJOY SWEET STRINGS
AT THE SYMPHONY

With eighty-three full-time professional musicians, the Milwaukee Symphony Orchestra is the largest cultural organization in the state. As Wisconsin's only professional orchestra, it has been a cornerstone of the Milwaukee arts community since 1959. Every year it presents more than 130 classical, pop, and educational concerts. A pioneer among American orchestras, it was the first American orchestra to offer live recordings on iTunes. It's obviously a great choice for anyone who appreciates the finer things in life, but classical music aficionados aren't the only people who will enjoy a trip to the symphony in Milwaukee. Concerts range from traditional favorites to fun modern performances featuring the music of Walt Disney, John Williams, and others. One of these pops shows might be the perfect way to introduce your family to the world of orchestra.

Family friendly, depending on concert

Milwaukee Symphony Orchestra
Marcus Center for the Performing Arts
929 N Water St., Milwaukee, WI 53202
mso.org

BASK
IN THE BALLET

There's nothing quite like the classical beauty of ballet. The Milwaukee Ballet, one of the nation's most celebrated companies, presents more than forty performances to more than fifty thousand people each year. Its productions range from classic favorites to new and innovative works. Attentive to global trends in theater, the company strives to put on at least one world premiere each year. You may have already seen the dancers of the Milwaukee Ballet at home; its wildly popular production of Peter Pan aired nationally on PBS. The company, which includes twenty-five professional dancers and twenty trainees, is one of the few dance companies in the country to maintain its own symphony orchestra. Kids love the annual performance of the *Nutcracker* in December, which features students from the Milwaukee Ballet School & Academy in the youth roles.

Milwaukee Ballet
Marcus Center for the Performing Arts
929 N Water St., Milwaukee, WI 53202
milwaukeeballet.org

SPORTS AND RECREATION

KAYAK
THROUGH THE CITY

There aren't a lot of cities you can explore from water level! The Milwaukee River winds through the city, joining the Kinnickinnic and Menomonee Rivers before flowing into Lake Michigan, and making the whole city a water wonderland. Rent a kayak from Milwaukee Kayak Company, and captain your own adventure on Milwaukee's rivers. You're free to explore any of the three rivers, but kayaking directly through downtown Milwaukee is probably the coolest option . . . even the most seasoned kayaker has never seen "rock formations" like these! This marriage of outdoor adventure and urban exploration is a unique and fun experience you won't soon forget. No kayaking experience is required; the Milwaukee Kayak Company staff will give you and your group a crash course before you hit the water.

Family friendly

Milwaukee Kayak Company
318 S Water St., Milwaukee, WI 53204
milwaukeekayak.com

CATCH A GAME
AT MILLER PARK

Miller Park, the home of the Milwaukee Brewers, has a distinctive retractable fan-shaped roof, which means that it's always perfect weather for a ball game. Your Miller Park experience begins with tailgating (a Milwaukee tradition) out in the stadium parking lot, located just minutes from downtown. Serious tailgaters will bring their grills, but it's just as fun to hang out with snacks or sandwiches and play some bean bag toss while you get revved up for the game. Once inside, you'll cheer on the famous Klement's Racing Sausages and join in a rousing rendition of "Roll Out the Barrel" during the seventh inning stretch. Hopefully the home team will hit a home run. When they do, you'll see team mascot Bernie Brewer take a celebratory trip down his slide.

Family friendly

Miller Park
1 Brewers Way, Milwaukee, WI 53214
milwaukee.brewers.mlb.com

EXPLORE
THE OAK LEAF TRAIL

Following the Oak Leaf Trail is a great way to explore the urban outdoors. This trail, more than one hundred miles long, encircles Milwaukee County, taking you on an urban (and not-so-urban) cycling adventure. While you're enjoying the tree-lined paths, you might even forget that some segments are practically in the heart of downtown. Go by bike or foot along the lakefront of Lake Michigan, through wooded sections alongside the Milwaukee River, and even along an abandoned railroad corridor. The ever-changing scenery along this paved trail system makes it a popular attraction for bikers, runners, rollerbladers, and walkers of all ages. The hardcore cyclist might make it a mission to bike the entire loop, while families will enjoy a leisurely stroll by the lake.

Family friendly

Oak Leaf Trail
county.milwaukee.gov/OakLeafTrail8289.htm

CHEER
ON THE BUCKS

Fear the deer! You'll catch fast-paced NBA action in the middle of downtown when the Milwaukee Bucks take the home court at the BMO Harris Bradley Center. As if the game on the court weren't exciting enough, each game has become a high-energy entertainment event that the whole family can enjoy. Bango, the team's mascot since 1977, is a fan favorite who's famous throughout the league. Bango shows off his acrobatic stunts, such as his back-flipping ladder dunk, at half time and performs his popular tricks at the NBA All-Star game each year. To imagine the excitement in the stadium, add in performances from the popular Bucks Dancers, the Bucks Beats Drumline, and the Rim Rockers, high-flying dunking daredevils. You can see that the action never stops, even when the players are off the court.

Family friendly

Milwaukee Bucks
BMO Harris Bradley Center
1001 N 4th St., Milwaukee, WI 53203
nba.com/bucks

PLAY BEACH VOLLEYBALL
ON BRADFORD BEACH

When you hear "beach volleyball," which cities come to mind? You probably only picture tropical locations, but don't leave Milwaukee off your list. Slap on some sunscreen and hit the beach! Bradford Beach, part of the Milwaukee County Parks System, is a thriving summertime hotspot, home to sunbathers, cabanas, and, yes, beach volleyball. Whether you're looking to play a match or just relax, Bradford Beach is the most popular beach in Milwaukee County and a big attraction to local players and leagues. Bradford Beach has hosted events such as the AVP Milwaukee Open Pro Beach Volleyball Tour and the USA Volleyball Junior Beach Tour Championships. While you're on the beach, stay fueled with snacks and beverages from the Bradford Beach Tiki Hut, which serves up classic concession snacks (tacos, hot dogs, burgers) alongside buckets of beer and island-ready mixed drinks.

Family friendly

Bradford Beach
2400 N Lincoln Memorial Dr,. Milwaukee, WI 53211
county.milwaukee.gov/Beaches9138.htm

TIP

After you've worked up an appetite,
enjoy a burger and cool treat from
Northpoint Custard, just off the sand.

GO SAILING
ON LAKE MICHIGAN

Set sail on Wisconsin's official flagship! The world's only recreation of a nineteenth-century Great Lakes schooner makes its home right here at Discovery World's Pier Wisconsin. A floating classroom, the S/V *Denis Sullivan* serves as an ambassador for the Great Lakes and freshwater concerns as it sails through the Great Lakes region, along the East Coast, and into the Caribbean. There are educational dockside and sailing expeditions for youth, but anyone who hears the call of the open water can participate in daytime or sunset sails on Lake Michigan. You can either sit back and enjoy the scenery, or become part of the crew to help set the sails and take your turn at the helm of this historic ship.

Family friendly

S/V *Denis Sullivan*
Discovery World
500 N Harbor Dr., Milwaukee, WI 53202
schoonerdenissullivan.org

EXPLORE
MILWAUKEE'S FREE OUTDOOR ART GALLERY

The three-mile-long Milwaukee RiverWalk is a continuous pedestrian walkway that follows the path of the Milwaukee River as it winds through downtown. This vibrant walkway offers the opportunity to take a scenic stroll from the Historic Third Ward, a revitalized warehouse district, through the downtown neighborhoods, and up to the historic Beerline B neighborhood. It's also home to "RiverSculpture!," a free outdoor art gallery. There are permanent pieces, such as the whimsical sculpture of Gertie, the world's most celebrated duck, as well as temporary installations. You'll see an average of twenty sculptures during your trek along the river. Many of Milwaukee's riverfront restaurants take advantage of their location for al fresco dining during the summer months, so don't forget to stop for lunch.

Family friendly

Milwaukee RiverWalk
milwaukeeriverwalkdistrict.com

ROOT
FOR ROLLER DERBY

There's nothing quite like the glittery, fishnet-covered action of roller derby. These ladies skate fast and hard, hitting the rink and each other in this fast-paced sport. You'll have to be quick witted to catch the wordplay in their clever derby nicknames as they're announced. The Brewcity Bruisers, the local league, is made up of four teams: Maiden Milwaukee, the Rushin' Rollettes, the Crazy 8's, and the Shevil Knevils. Each match is a double header; you'll get to see all four teams skating at breakneck pace around the track. Bouts are family friendly, but be forewarned that you have to be eighteen to sit on the floor next to the track. You may end up with a lapful of flying rollergirl!

Family friendly

Brewcity Bruisers
UW-Milwaukee Panther Arena
400 W Kilbourn Ave., Milwaukee, WI 53203
brewcitybruisers.com

EXPLORE THE CITY
ON TWO WHEELS

Whether you're a devoted cyclist or just looking for a new way to get around, you don't have to bring a bike with you to cycle around the city. Bike share systems are popping up all across the country, and Milwaukee is no exception. Named after the uniquely Milwaukee word for a drinking fountain, the cheery blue Bublr Bikes are a fun and easy way to explore the city. Riding a bike connects you to the environment in a way that driving through the city doesn't, and you can travel farther and faster than you can on foot. Plus, it's just plain fun! You can't beat a leisurely bike ride along the lakefront or a quick trip to a new restaurant for lunch. The stations connect some of the city's most popular thoroughfares and attractions, making it easy to rent a bike for a short amount of time.

Family friendly (14+)

Bublr Bikes
Various locations
bublrbikes.com

BOWL
AT HOLLER HOUSE

The oldest certified bowling alley in America is found in one of Milwaukee's classic corner taverns. The planks on these two old-time lanes are made of real wood, unlike the synthetic material that makes up modern bowling lanes. The pins are still set by human pinsetters, and you better brush up on keeping score by hand. Open since 1908, Holler House is iconic old Milwaukee and was ranked by *Esquire* as one of the best bars in America. It's still run by Marcy Skowronski, the daughter-in-law of the original owner. The bowling alley is not the only sight to see in this tavern. You'll find the bar bedecked by the brassieres of past patrons; women are encouraged to leave a bra behind on their first visit.

Holler House
2042 W Lincoln Ave., Milwaukee, WI 53215

TIP

If you plan to bowl,
call ahead to make sure
a pinsetter is on duty.

RELAX
ON A RIVER CRUISE

What could be better on a nice warm day than a boat ride? Don't miss the chance to see the city from the water. Whether you prefer a historic informational boat ride the whole family will enjoy or a happy hour cocktail cruise for a group of friends, find a river cruise and cast off for some relaxation on the water. These boats will take you along the Milwaukee River and through the harbor, offering a stunning view of Milwaukee from Lake Michigan. Many boats offer enclosed sections where you can remain unruffled by the wind, but where's the fun in that? Soak in the sunshine and enjoy the breeze from the lake while you float down the river.

Family friendly, depending on cruise

Milwaukee River Cruise Line
205 W Highland Ave., #204, Milwaukee, WI 53203
edelweissboats.com

Milwaukee Boat Line
101 W Michigan St., Milwaukee, WI 53203
mkeboat.com

GO ON
A PEDALING PUB CRAWL

Don't think that beer and exercise go together? They do in Milwaukee! Milwaukee's only pedaling pub crawl is a great way to explore the city's nightlife and get a workout at the same time. Climb aboard the sixteen-person bike to pedal your way through the Historic Third Ward and Walker's Point neighborhoods. You'll make stops to take advantage of exclusive drink specials at all of the most popular watering holes. Join a public pub crawl, or rent the whole bike for a private tour of the bars of your choice. A friendly Pedal Tavern staff member is there to "drive" the bike, so all you need to worry about is providing the leg power (and stocking the onboard cooler)!

Pedal Tavern
800 S 2nd St., Milwaukee, WI 53202
pedaltavern.com

GO FLY A KITE

A clear blue sky over the sparkling blue water of Lake Michigan is beautiful . . . but it's even more lovely with the addition of brightly colored kites! Didn't think to bring one along? No problem! Gift of Wings is Milwaukee's only full-service kite shop, and it's conveniently located in Veterans Park right on the lakefront. Stop in on a breezy day to pick out a kite, many of which are original designs created right here in Milwaukee, or come for one of the kite festivals held throughout the year. Families can help kick off the event with the grand kite launch, then enjoy the show as master performers show off their routines and giant kites take over the sky.

Family friendly

Gift of Wings
Veterans Park
1300 N Lincoln Memorial D., Milwaukee, WI 53202
giftofwings.com

CHECK OUT
A 24-HOUR BIKE RACE

If you're a passionate cyclist, how about trying a race that lasts for twenty-four hours? Created to celebrate the community of Milwaukee's Riverwest neighborhood and encourage urban biking, the Riverwest 24 is an event unlike any other. The goal is to make as many laps as possible in the twenty-four-hour period. Riders can earn bonus laps by participating in checkpoint challenges, such as going down a Slip 'N Slide, taking a dance break, and getting a Riverwest 24 tattoo. Some racers are dedicated cyclists with their eye on the prize, and some dress in zany costumes, just looking to have a good time. You don't have to be a cyclist to get in on the fun; the race also serves as a twenty-four-hour carnival/block party as the whole community comes out to celebrate and cheer on the riders. With food trucks, music, entertainment, and local businesses that stay open for the entire event, the Riverwest 24 is part race, part party, part movement, and a full twenty-four hours of fun.

Riverwest 24
riverwest24.com

EXPLORE
THE URBAN OUTDOORS

Get in touch with nature without ever leaving the city! The Urban Ecology Center, with three locations, is dedicated to restoring urban green spaces, providing ecological education, and offering free, fun ways to interact with nature. The original location in Riverside Park is a "green" building like you've never seen before. Built with environmental features like rainwater flush toilets and a green roof garden, this building houses one of the largest solar power stations in Wisconsin. The designers didn't forget to add a few special features just for fun, such as the tower with a forty-foot climbing wall and the secret slide entrance. In a habitat-themed playground, kids can climb a spider web, play in the woodland dunes sandbox, and slide down otter slides.

Family friendly

Urban Ecology Center: Riverside Park
1500 E Park Place, Milwaukee, WI 53211
urbanecologycenter.org

GO ICE SKATING
DOWNTOWN

There's no more magical winter experience than ice skating downtown among the twinkling lights of the city. Milwaukee's favorite place to skate is Slice of Ice, an outdoor refrigerated rink in Red Arrow Park, located in the heart of the city and across from the beautiful multicolored lights of the Marcus Center for the Performing Arts. Open from December to February (or March, depending on the weather), you only have to pay to rent your skates; if you bring your own, you skate for free! Plus, take advantage of the warming house after your romp on the ice. Here you can enjoy the heat, restrooms, and Starbucks coffee and pastries available for purchase. The floor-to-ceiling windows give you a great view of the ice.

Family friendly

Slice of Ice
Red Arrow Park
920 N Water St., Milwaukee, WI 53202
county.milwaukee.gov/RedArrow11930.htm

CHEER ON ROWING TEAMS
ON THE MILWAUKEE RIVER

Dozens of collegiate and club rowing teams take to the Milwaukee and Menomonee Rivers each fall for the Milwaukee River Challenge. This three-mile race, which includes a difficult ninety-degree turn as participants move from the Menomonee River into the Milwaukee River, tests both speed and precision. Thanks to the Milwaukee RiverWalk and the dozens of bridges that span the river, this race is a unique opportunity for spectators to get an intimate look at the regatta. You'll be close enough to see the water droplets flying as the teams race their way through the city. Catch all the action in the staging area at Schlitz Park, or refer to the website to find the best locations for spectators along the race route.

Family friendly

Milwaukee River Challenge
Starts at 25th and Canal St.
milwaukeeriverchallenge.com

BE A PACKER BACKER

Green Bay may be two hours away, but don't ever try to tell Milwaukeeans that the Packers aren't their team. Around here, those are fighting words! The city goes green and gold on game days, and many bars offer drink specials, free food, and other perks. So grab a cheesehead (yes, we actually wear those big foam hats made of cheese) and join in the fun. Although pretty much every bar in the city becomes a Packers bar on game day, here are a few popular spots to catch the action. Major Goolsby's is Milwaukee's most iconic sports bar; it has served up its famous flame-broiled burgers for more than forty years. Though it's newer on the scene, Camp Bar, with its rustic cabin theme, has quickly become a local favorite.

Major Goolsby's
340 W Kilbourn Ave., Milwaukee, WI 53203
majorgoolsbys.com

Camp Bar
4044 N Oakland Ave., Shorewood, WI 53211
campbarmke.co

DO THE WAVE
FOR THE WAVE

You don't have to wait for the World Cup to come around again to get excited about soccer! The Milwaukee Wave is the oldest continually operating professional soccer franchise in North America. It brings fast-paced indoor soccer to the UW-Milwaukee Panther Arena. Six-time champions, the Wave reliably offer a high scoring, exciting sports experience. Each game is guaranteed fun (no, really, it's guaranteed!) with tons of giveaways, theme nights, and interactive fan experiences for all ages. If you make it onto the field, you might have to carry a keg through an obstacle course, show off your best dance moves, or even roll yourself across the field in a mattress. Bring your vuvuzela and cheer on the Wave!

Family friendly

The Wave
UW-Milwaukee Panther Arena
400 W Kilbourn Ave., Milwaukee, WI 53203
milwaukeewave.com

MEET THE RAPTORS

The Schlitz Audubon Nature Center, originally a farm for Schlitz Brewery draft horses, is a comprehensive nature center located just outside the city. Their one hundred and eighty-five acre grounds include forests, wetlands, restored prairies, ravines, bluffs, and shoreline. All can be explored via six miles of hiking trails or admired from atop a sixty-foot observation tower that offers one of the best views in the area. Schlitz Audubon is a great place to explore the variety of Wisconsin's natural spaces, but it's probably most popular for its educational wildlife programs. During their popular raptor program, you can get up close and personal with live birds of prey, including hawks, owls, falcons, a turkey vulture, and an American crow. All the birds featured in the program are permanent residents of the center that cannot be released due to injury.

Family friendly

Schlitz Audubon Nature Center
1111 E Brown Deer Rd., Milwaukee, WI 53217
schlitzaudubon.org

WATCH THE ADS
TAKE THE ICE

Ahoy, hockey fans! Originally founded as an amateur team in 1970, the Milwaukee Admirals are now a member of the American Hockey League and the top affiliate of the NHL's Nashville Predators. The Ads, as they're known to locals, are one of the city's best sports values and always a favorite team for families. Enjoy lightning-fast action on the ice along with fun intermission contests like Uncle Ben's Human Hockey Puck, which slingshots a lucky fan across the ice on a sled. If you're lucky, you just might end up catching a ride on the zamboni! As if that weren't enough, the Ads bring great bands to the arena by regularly hosting concerts immediately after select games.

Family friendly

Milwaukee Admirals
BMO Harris Bradley Center
1001 N 4th St., Milwaukee, WI 53203
milwaukeeadmirals.com

CULTURE AND HISTORY

VISIT
THE WORLD'S SEXIEST BUILDING

It's not often that the structure that houses an art collection can compare to the beauty of what's inside. The Milwaukee Art Museum, designed by Santiago Calatrava, is the jewel of Milwaukee's lakefront and was named the "sexiest building in the world." Designed to be a "post-modern Gothic cathedral," the soaring ninety-foot ceilings are breathtaking, as are the giant "wings" of the Burke Brise Soleil. Inside the lobby, you'll be stunned by a colorful Dale Chihuly sculpture. Explore a collection of over thirty thousand works of art, including some of the nation's best holdings of American decorative arts, German expressionism, folk and Haitian art, and American art after 1960. The museum also holds one of the largest collections of work by Wisconsin native Georgia O'Keeffe. The Milwaukee County War Memorial Center, designed by Eero Saarinen, is also part of the Milwaukee Art Museum campus.

Family friendly

Milwaukee Art Museum
700 N Art Museum Dr., Milwaukee, WI 53202
mam.org

TIP

Catch the "wings" of the museum open in the morning, flap at noon and close at sunset (weather permitting).

DISCOVER
DISCOVERY WORLD

New technology meets maritime history at this popular interactive museum celebrating science, water, and innovation. Take a totally immersive three-dimensional virtual reality journey inside the H.I.V.E, lie on a bed of nails, and check out a "hair-raising" Van de Graaff generator. Then, explore the inside of a nuclear reactor to learn about different forms of energy. Les Paul's House of Sound gives you an inside look at the collection of the innovative musician and inventor, including more than twenty new guitars and never-before-seen memorabilia. If you've come for the water, the Reiman Aquarium is home to wildlife from the Great Lakes, North Atlantic, and Caribbean. You can get up close and personal with stingrays, sturgeons, and other creatures in the Touch Tank. You can even climb aboard the Challenge, a life-size recreation of an 1852 schooner.

Family friendly

Discovery World
500 N Harbor Dr., Milwaukee, WI 532024
discoveryworld.org

VISIT THE STREETS
OF OLD MILWAUKEE

Home to more than four and half million specimens, the Milwaukee Public Museum explores the intersection of natural science and human history. Travel around the world, observing the crafts and cultures of Africa, Asia, Europe, the Arctic, South and Middle America, and the Pacific Islands. You can even experience a Costa Rican rainforest. See the depths of the ocean, or go back sixty-five million years by viewing one of the world's oldest dinosaur skulls. You can literally take a stroll through Milwaukee's past in the iconic Streets of Old Milwaukee exhibit; there you'll see the start of some of the brands and companies that remain in the city today. Interact with live butterflies year-round in the Puelicher Butterfly Wing, see a film in the dome theater, and explore traveling special exhibits.

Family friendly

Milwaukee Public Museum
800 W Wells St., Milwaukee, WI 53233
mpm.edu

SEE HOW
THE BEER BARONS LIVED

The Pabst Mansion, built in 1892 by beer baron Captain Frederick Pabst, is a jewel of America's Gilded Age. What began as a private residence and became the center of the Archdiocese of Milwaukee is now one of the nation's foremost house museums. Take a guided tour through this historic showpiece home, open daily, to see where Milwaukee's elite were once entertained by the Pabst family. In addition to its stunning collection of decorative and fine arts, the Pabst Mansion has thirty-seven rooms, twelve bathrooms, and fourteen fireplaces. The house has been beautifully restored with period details based on original photography of the interior rooms. The mansion is especially famous for its stunning Christmas decorations, an elegant holiday display that's bound to transport you to another time.

Family friendly

Pabst Mansion
2000 W Wisconsin Ave., Milwaukee, WI 53233
pabstmansion.com

EXPERIENCE ART
IN NATURE

Lynden Sculpture Garden is a unique outdoor gallery that houses a collection of more than fifty monumental sculptures on forty acres of park, lake, and woodland. Purchased as a private residence in 1927, Lynden was opened to the public in 2010. At that time, the house and grounds were extensively renovated to add a gallery, classrooms, and eco-sensitive landscaping. The collection of sculptures coexists with the natural ecology of the site. There are no paths at Lynden; visitors are welcome to wander and explore the stunning collection of contemporary sculpture. You can expect to see pieces by Alexander Archipenko, Henry Moore, Barbara Hepworth, Clement Meadmore, Marta Pan, Tony Smith, and Mark di Suvero. If you'd like to learn more, there are docent-led tours each Sunday.

Family friendly

Lynden Sculpture Garden
2145 W Brown Deer Rd., Milwaukee, WI 53217
lyndensculpturegarden.org

TRAVEL THE
HORTICULTURAL WORLD

Did you know you can visit the desert and the jungle without leaving the city limits? The three eighty-five-foot-high conoidal domes that make up the Mitchell Park Conservatory (and give it its local nickname "The Domes") are the only ones of their kind in the world. They're a striking sight that might make you want to linger outside to gawk, but the fun really starts blooming once you walk through the doors. The arid Desert Dome is home to one of the world's finest collections of cacti, succulents, and shrubs. It brings you to the deserts of Africa, Madagascar, and North and South America. The Tropical Dome is full of showy flowers, fruits, nuts, and spices. Colorful birds live among these jungle plants. The Floral Show Dome, which features five themed seasonal displays each year, is always a popular site during the holidays.

Mitchell Park Horticultural Conservatory
524 S Layton Blvd. Milwaukee, WI 53215
milwaukeedomes.org

CELEBRATE ART
ON GALLERY NIGHT

Perhaps you're an art lover who prefers to enjoy a painting or sculpture with a glass of wine in hand or whilst hobnobbing with local artists. You'll feel right at home at Gallery Night & Day! More than sixty venues open their doors during Milwaukee's premiere art event, held quarterly by the Historic Third Ward. Both new art admirers and experienced connoisseurs will find something to love during this vibrant free event. Galleries and other local venues throughout downtown present special exhibitions, art installations, food, live music, interactive projects, and more on Friday night. The fun continues, but with limited options, during the day on Saturday. Plan to make a night of it and enjoy dinner, drinks, and dessert at various restaurants; free shuttle buses will help you hit all the venues.

Gallery Night & Day
Various venues
historicthirdward.org/events/gallerynight.php

STEP BEHIND THE SCENES
AT HISTORIC BUILDINGS

Have you ever wanted to see what goes on behind closed doors? Doors Open is one big behind-the-scenes tour for the whole city, which takes you to the places that only locals know . . . and that even they have probably never seen in person! This free event, presented by Historic Milwaukee, lets you tour and explore some of the city's most fascinating buildings, several of which are open to the public for this weekend only. From churches to theaters, hotels to office buildings, see the hidden treasures and learn the special stories of more than one hundred and fifty architecturally, historically, and culturally relevant sites. In addition to the free "open door" tours, select sites also offer ticketed in-depth tours led by an expert if you have a special interest.

Family friendly

Doors Open
Various locations
doorsopenmilwaukee.org

PAY YOUR RESPECTS
TO MILWAUKEE'S LATE GREATS

The two hundred tranquil, park-like acres of Forest Home Cemetery are the final resting place to a veritable "who's who" of Milwaukee's late greats. The cemetery is listed on the National Register of Historic Places and is a designated Milwaukee landmark for its historical significance. It may seem a bit morbid, but there's a lot to be learned on the self-guided walking tour of this cemetery. The Victorian landscape includes over three hundred species of trees, and the dearly departed of old have filled it with ornate statues, crypts, and monuments. Pay your respects to twenty-eight Milwaukee mayors, seven Wisconsin governors, three beer barons, the founders of Harley-Davidson, noted industrialists, activists, and others. During your visit, stop by the Halls of History to learn more about the history of Milwaukee.

Forest Home Cemetery
2405 Forest Home Ave., Milwaukee, WI 53215
foresthomecemetery.com

TOUR
THE BASILICA

Completed in 1901, the Basilica of St. Josaphat was built in the style of St. Peter's in Rome and is still the largest church in Milwaukee. They didn't label it "sustainable" in those days, but St. Josaphat was built with salvaged materials from the recently demolished Chicago Post Office. At the time of completion, the only building in the country with a larger dome was the United States Capitol. In the Catholic Church, the title "basilica" is reserved for the most beautiful and historically important churches. In 1929, St. Josaphat's became the third basilica in the United States. If you want to view the stained glass windows and oil murals, the basilica is open to the public for self-guided walking tours throughout the week. A formal guided tour is available after Sunday Mass.

Basilica of St. Josaphat
2333 S 6th St., Milwaukee, WI 53215
thebasilica.org

WALK THROUGH
MILWAUKEE'S HISTORY

When you're exploring Milwaukee on foot or by car, you'll see a wide variety of historic buildings and beautiful architecture. If you're the type who wants to know more about a building's history or wonders why none of the bridges in Milwaukee make a straight connection across the river (for example), join Historic Milwaukee for a walking tour. The walking tour is a fun and affordable way to learn more about the city and find answers to all of your questions. The downtown tour gives you a crash course in Milwaukee's history. It takes you, both literally and figuratively, from the city's earliest origins to its most stunning modern building, the Milwaukee Art Museum. Historic Milwaukee also offers a variety of themed neighborhood tours and a winter tour that takes place entirely in Milwaukee's skywalk system.

Family friendly

Historic Milwaukee
Various locations
historicmilwaukee.org/tours/walking-tours

VISIT
A MEDIEVAL CHURCH

Constructed in France during the late fourteenth or early fifteenth century, the St. Joan of Arc Chapel is the only known medieval building in the western hemisphere still used for its original purpose. Originally part of a chateau belonging to a prominent French family near the city of Lyon, the chapel fell into disrepair after the French Revolution. In 1926, it was brought to America stone by stone and reconstructed on an estate in New York. In 1964 it was presented to Marquette University. The chapel's second reconstruction was completed on the Marquette University campus in 1966, at which point it was dedicated to St. Joan of Arc. Mass is still held in this historic chapel while classes are in session, and tours are available throughout the week.

St. Joan of Arc Chapel
1335 W Wisconsin Ave., Milwaukee, WI 53233
(Located behind the Memorial Library)
marquette.edu/chapel

EXPLORE
THE ORIGINAL SOLDIERS HOME

Milwaukee's Soldiers Home, built in 1867 to house recovering soldiers after the Civil War, is the most intact of the three original Soldiers Homes in the country; it is the only one that retains the majority of its recuperative village. The original domiciliary, Old Main, sits at the highest point of the campus. The surrounding buildings, once a village whose purpose was to care for the recuperating veterans, include a theater where Bob Hope and Liberace once performed. In 2012, the Milwaukee Soldiers Home was named one of the National Trust for Historic Preservation's National Treasures. Ongoing restoration continues to preserve and repair this historical treasure. Visitors can download a free self-guided audio walking tour to help learn more about this hidden jewel, and support its preservation.

Soldiers Home
5000 W National Ave., Milwaukee, WI 53295
savethesoldiershome.com

EXPLORE THE HIDDEN GEMS
OF THE MUSEUM SCENE

The Milwaukee Museum Mile is a unique consortium that links five small local museums. The Jewish Museum Milwaukee presents the history and culture of American Jews, particularly in southeastern Wisconsin and Milwaukee. The Charles Allis Art Museum is a lavish Tudor-style home that holds an art collection spanning more than two thousand years. Its sister museum, Villa Terrace Decorative Arts Museum, which is built inside an Italian Renaissance–style villa, features fine and decorative arts as well as a beautiful formal garden. North Point Lighthouse offers a look into Milwaukee's maritime past as well as a stunning panoramic view of the city. Finally, the Museum of Wisconsin Art at St. John's on the Lake holds the preeminent collection of the visual art of Wisconsin.

Family friendly

milwaukeemuseummile.org

TIP
Present your Milwaukee Museum Mile brochure to receive $1 off admission at each destination.

MEMORABLE MUSEUMS

Jewish Museum Milwaukee
1360 N Prospect Ave., Milwaukee, WI 53202
jewishmuseummilwaukee.org

Charles Allis Art Museum
1801 N Prospect Ave., Milwaukee, WI 53202
charlesallis.org

Villa Terrace Decorative Arts Museum
2220 N Terrace Ave., Milwaukee, WI 53202
villaterracemuseum.org

North Point Lighthouse
2650 N Wahl Ave., Milwaukee, WI
northpointlighthouse.org

Museum of Wisconsin Art
205 Veterans Ave., West Bend, WI 53095
wisconsinart.org

TOUR
CENTRAL LIBRARY

You might be struck by a massive stone structure built in Renaissance style in downtown Milwaukee. Could it be another impressive mansion? With its limestone walls and fancy columns, very few people would guess that this colossal structure is actually the headquarters of the Milwaukee Public Library system! A designated Milwaukee landmark, Central Library is one of downtown's most monumental public structures. The original structure was built in 1898 in a combination of French and Italian Renaissance styles. In the years since, it has expanded into the block-long building that exists today. The library features restored hand-laid mosaic tile floors, a newly installed green roof that spans thirty-three thousand square feet, and, of course, an impressive collection of books. Visitors can tour this historic building for free each week.

Family friendly

Central Library
814 W Wisconsin Ave., Milwaukee, WI 53233
mpl.org/hours_locations/central.php

SEE ALL THE BEST
ON A CITY TOUR

If you're in town for a short period of time or just love an all-in-one experience, Untapped Tours is your best bet for seeing the "greatest hits" (and a few hidden gems) of Milwaukee in one fell swoop. Best of all, you don't need to worry about transportation. Drive through Milwaukee's history while making great stops, such as at the Milwaukee Art Museum, Lakefront Brewery (complete with a beer sample!), Miller Park, and Clock Shadow Creamery (yup, you get to try some cheese). You can see it all on this three hour guided tour, complete with plenty of breaks for photos and interaction with the locals. The tours are limited to eleven guests, which makes each experience personal and permits plenty of room to stretch out and explore.

Untapped Tours
untappedtours.com

GET TO WORK
AT THE GROHMANN

If there's one thing we can all relate to, it's work. The Grohmann Museum, one of Milwaukee's hidden museum treasures, is home to the world's largest art collection dedicated to the evolution of human work. The collection is composed of more than one thousand paintings and sculptures ranging from 1580 to the present, representing a number of styles and subjects. See how the nature of "work" changes, starting with depictions of life on the farm or at home, transitioning to trades like blacksmith or cobbler, and ending with massive industrial machines. The museum is located in a three-story concrete structure on the campus of the Milwaukee School of Engineering. It was originally built in 1924 as an automobile dealership and more recently served as the Federal Reserve Bank.

Grohmann Museum
1000 N Broadway, Milwaukee, WI 53202
msoe.edu/community/about-msoe/grohmann-museum

TAKE IN BEAUTIFUL HOMES
IN NORTH POINT

Though located just two miles from the bustle of downtown, Milwaukee's North Point neighborhood almost feels like a step into another world. There are nearly four hundred houses in North Point, and they represent the work of Milwaukee's finest architects and craftspeople from days past. These stunning architectural gems showcase a number of styles, from English Tudor to Mediterranean and French Renaissance, and even include a home designed by Frank Lloyd Wright. Villa Terrace, now a museum, is the only home and garden open to the public, but the beauty of this neighborhood is well worth exploring whether by car or on foot. Bring a picnic to enjoy in one of the local parks. After your feast, take a stroll through this historic neighborhood.

North Point
hwtn.org

LEARN
ABOUT URBAN FARMING

Farm-to-table cuisine is a growing movement, but here in Milwaukee, the farm might be even closer than you thought. Growing Power's urban farm is the last remaining farm and greenhouse in operation in the city of Milwaukee. Devoted to urban agriculture, sustainable food systems, and support for the local community, Growing Power is both an operating farm and an outreach program. As part of their outreach, they provide sustainable food and job training to underserved youth. You can tour the farm and learn more about the sustainable growing methods they use. Practices include using worms to compost the waste, fish to fertilize the plants, and honeybees to pollinate the flowers in the neighborhood. Growing Power supplies produce to many local restaurants; before you go out to eat, make a stop to see where it all happens.

Family friendly

Growing Power
5500 W Silver Spring Dr., Milwaukee, WI 53218
growingpower.org

FIND
MILWAUKEE MURALS

Milwaukee's murals are as vibrant and diverse as the city itself. It can be hard to track down public art throughout a city when you don't know where to look. Luckily, the Milwaukee Mural Map is an ongoing project devoted to documenting the city's murals. From the north side to the south side, this is the easiest way to track down Milwaukee's beautiful outdoor art. These murals offer a peek inside the mind of the city and its artists, bringing you ever closer to its heart. Take yourself on a self-guided tour of art in the city using the digital map as a resource to provide more information about the murals you see along the way. You can even find suggested bike tour routes through the areas that are most heavily populated with murals.

Family friendly

Milwaukee Mural Map
mkemuralmap.com

SHOPPING
AND FASHION

FIND ARTS AND STYLE
IN THE HISTORIC THIRD WARD

Known as the "SoHo" of Milwaukee, the Historic Third Ward is the home of arts and fashion. Here, warehouses have been revitalized and repurposed into trendy shops and galleries that sell everything from designer clothing to artisan chocolates, stylish eyewear to unique jewelry. Visit Broadway Paper, a charming stationery store that's a must-stop for anyone in search of lovely cards, office supplies, and gifts. Need a new pair of jeans? Denim Bar MKE features one thousand pairs of premium jeans, the largest selection of denim in Wisconsin. Locally owned gallery and boutique Hot*Pop is the perfect place for quirky home goods or gifts as well as pieces by local artists. This neighborhood is also home to major national retailers, such as Anthropologie, West Elm, and Pendleton.

Broadway Paper
191 N Broadway, Milwaukee, WI 53202
broadwaypaper.com

Denim Bar MKE
317 N Broadway, Milwaukee, WI 53202
denimbarmke.com

Hot*Pop
201 N Water St., Milwaukee, WI 53202
hotpopshop.com

PICK OUT
A DASHING HAT

Return to the dapper days of old at Milwaukee's premiere hat shop. In addition to selling hats from top brands like Bailey, Broener, DPC, Stetson, and Dobbs, the Brass Rooster also offers its own line of hats. All of their hats are handmade the traditional way on equipment that's more than eighty years old. You can even commission an entirely custom cap if nothing in the store catches your eye. After picking out the proper hat, a gentleman will find in this shop everything he needs to look sharp. Merchandise includes the Brass Rooster line of shave and body soap, pomade, mustache wax, vintage belt buckles, and more. Don't worry, ladies . . . you'll find everything you need for retro glamour right next door in their women's shop, The Hen House.

Brass Rooster/The Hen House
2250 S Kinnickinnic Ave., Milwaukee, WI 53207
brassrooster.com

GET LOST
IN ANTIQUES ON SECOND

You can certainly go to Antiques on Second on a mission for a specific item, but it's much more fun to keep an open mind. With more than two hundred vendors showing their wares in a space that encompasses more than forty thousand square feet, you'll want to set aside a few hours to comb through this local gem. The selection is incredible. This is not your grandmother's antique mall; in the various displays, you'll find everything from vintage clothing, jewelry, decor, and furniture to creative taxidermy and pop culture memorabilia. There's a notable selection of Wisconsin books and maps. You're even welcome to enjoy complimentary cookies and coffee while you browse. It's no surprise this has been voted Milwaukee's best antique store for several years running.

Antiques on Second
1039 S. 2nd Street, Milwaukee, WI 53204
antiquesonsecond.com

Note: Antiques on Second will be moving soon.
Check their website for an updated address.

STROLL
THROUGH CHARMING CEDARBURG

Cedarburg, located just north of Milwaukee, is a charming village full of boutiques and a well-known shopping destination. There are around seventy specialty shops, boutiques, and galleries in the historic downtown district alone. Spend a day strolling through the neighborhood to see what you'll find. Stores stock everything from antiques to art and gardening supplies to sweet treats. Make sure to stop in at the Shops of Cedar Creek Settlement, a grand stone complex that was built in 1864 as a mill to produce woolen products. The settlement now houses more than thirty shops and restaurants, including the award-winning Cedar Creek Winery. Cedarburg hosts several family-friendly seasonal festivals throughout the year, including a very popular Strawberry Festival in summer. Definitely take advantage of those special events if they coincide with your visit.

Family friendly

Cedar Creek Settlement
6340 Bridge Rd., Cedarburg, WI 53012
cedarcreeksettlement.com

FIND GERMAN HERITAGE
ON OLD WORLD THIRD STREET

Old World Third Street was the center of Milwaukee's German population, and it's still the best place to go if you're looking for a little bit of all things Deutsch. On the second floor of Mader's Restaurant, you'll find hundreds of beer steins direct from Germany, including a few antique steins. Mader's, also America's largest Hummel store, has thousands of M. J. Hummel figurines in stock, including exclusively decorated Hummels and priceless original charcoal pastels. If you're more interested in picking up some snacks to take home, stop by Usinger's Famous Sausage, where the Usinger family has been making their one-of-a-kind sausages for over 130 years. Their wurstmachers are still located on Old World Third Street, the site of the original store. They use the original family recipes, unchanged since 1880. Pick up some cheese to go with that sausage at Wisconsin Cheese Mart, which has housed the world's largest selection of Wisconsin cheese since 1938.

Family friendly

YOU'LL WANT TO VISIT

Mader's
1041 N Old World Third St.
Milwaukee, WI 53203
madersrestaurant.com

Usinger's Famous Sausage
1030 N Old World Third St.
Milwaukee, WI 53203
usinger.com

Wisconsin Cheese Mart
215 W Highland Ave.
Milwaukee, WI 53203
wisconsincheesemart.com

SHOP LOCAL
AT SPARROW COLLECTIVE

There's a treasure trove inside a sliver of a gift shop in the eclectic Bay View neighborhood. You would never guess the breadth of their collection from the outside, but this tiny little shop somehow manages to contain the work of more than one hundred independent designers from all across the country, including several local Milwaukee creators. The designs and products for sale are always changing, but you're sure to find something fabulous no matter what's on offer. This is one of the city's best stops if you're looking for a gift, but have not quite decided what to get. It has been locally voted "Best Gift Shop." On any given visit you're likely to find cutting boards, homemade soap, pottery, art prints, jewelry, stylish clothes, baby gifts, coasters, and so much more.

Sparrow Collective
2224 S Kinnickinnic Ave., Milwaukee, WI 53207
sparrowcollective.com

SHOP
FOR ITALIAN FAVORITES

Ciao, bella! Milwaukee may be most famous for its German heritage, but the city is actually a melting pot of cultures that welcomed immigrants from all over the globe. Glorioso's Italian Market, family-owned since 1946, is still Milwaukee's source for everything Italian. It anchors Brady Street, which was once the home of Milwaukee's Italian population. Glorioso's has continuously been voted the city's favorite deli and has been nationally recognized as the thirteenth spot on Travel Channel's "101 Amazing Places to Chowdown." You can pick up a great lunch at their deli counter, which serves up everything from calzones to fresh pasta. You'll also find all of the imported treats you might need to create an Italian feast. Munch on a scoop of gelato while you explore the fresh and frozen pasta, imported meats and cheeses, olives, wine, and other delicacies.

Family friendly

Glorioso's Italian Market
1011 E Brady St., Milwaukee, WI 53202
gloriosos.com

TAKE HOME
SOME BEER MEMORABILIA

If you need a souvenir to remember your time in the city, purchasing something beer-themed is a no-brainer. The Girl in the Moon Brewery Shop in the Miller Visitor Center sells everything from T-shirts to neon signs; you can also pick up custom glassware only available here. If retro brews are more your style, the gift shop at Best Place at the Pabst Brewery sells articles directly recovered from the Pabst Brewery. Memorabilia includes original stock certificates, promotional materials, and vintage postcards. And, of course, the best beer-themed souvenir is, well, beer! You don't have to leave behind the local brews you fell in love with during your trip—grab a six pack to take home with you!

The Girl in the Moon Brewery Shop
4251 W State St., Milwaukee, WI 53208
millercoors.com/Brewery-Tours/Milwaukee-Brewery-Tour/Gift-Shop

Best Place
901 W Juneau Ave., Milwaukee, WI 53233
bestplacemilwaukee.com/giftshop.html

GET HIP
AT INDIE CRAFT FAIRS

There's a whole new breed of craft fairs, and Milwaukee is full of them. It's no surprise that a city with such strong industrial roots is still home to a hearty do-it-yourself spirit. You'll find shoppers of all ages checking out local makers that sell everything from upcycled vintage furniture to baby hats. It's not all kitsch and quilts, though you'll find plenty of both! Even if you're not looking to buy, Milwaukee's indie craft fairs are great places to people watch and appreciate creativity! Hover Craft is one of the biggest and most popular single shows of the year. You'll find maker markets throughout the summer and curated vendors at street fairs and events year-round.

Family friendly

Hover Craft
hovercraftmke.blogspot.com

Maker Market
makermarketmke.com

FIND WHAT YOU DIDN'T KNOW
YOU WERE LOOKING FOR

There's a store in Milwaukee that's perfect for everyone from little kids to grown-ups who still think they're kids. You never know what you might find at American Science & Surplus, located on the city's south side. With military, educational, and scientific items on offer, you'll see everything from ammo chests to a truly impressive array of test tubes. Reading the creative, humorous descriptions of the wacky items are just as much fun as discovering them. You might pick up a fun science kit or some tools or a bit of rope or goggles or a labcoat or the perfect prank. Whether you're a tinkerer, an inventor, a do-it-yourselfer, or just a curious soul, you'll find an unexpected treasure at this unique store.

Family friendly

American Science & Surplus
6901 W Oklahoma Ave., Milwaukee, WI 53219
sciplus.com

SUPPORT
LOCAL FARMERS
ALL YEAR

You don't have to miss out on the farmers' market experience just because you're visiting during the winter months! The Milwaukee County Winter Farmers Market, which runs on Saturday mornings from November to April, is the place to find local and sustainable food when other markets are closed for the season. More than thirty vendors attend each week, bringing fruit, vegetables, meat, eggs, and dairy products. Some vendors offer prepared items, such as baked goods, jams, honey, soups, and other delicious goodies to this free indoor marketplace. All of the vendors live within ninety miles of the market, making this a truly local operation. Buy a snack from one of the food vendors to tide you over while you explore the bounty on offer. It'll make you forget that it's cold outside!

Milwaukee County Winter Farmers Market
524 S Layton Blvd., Milwaukee, WI 53215
mcwfm.org

WANDER
IN WAUWATOSA

Some of the area's best shopping is found just west of the city in Wauwatosa. Everyone can find something to bring home from these major shopping centers, packed with popular national brands as well as chic boutiques. The largest shopping center in Wisconsin is Mayfair Mall, home to many popular brands and the state's only Nordstrom. If you're looking for independent shopping in Tosa, as locals call it, head over to the Village in Wauwatosa, the historic European village center. This walkable district is filled with more than one hundred stores, restaurants, and businesses selling everything from designer fashion to bath and body products. Take a day to walk around the area, and make sure to save time in between your shopping stops for some lunch! Pizzeria Piccola is a great casual lunch spot that serves up wood-fired personal pizzas.

Family friendly

WHAT TO SEE IN WAUWATOSA

Mayfair Mall
2500 N Mayfair Rd.
Wauwatosa, WI 53226
mayfairmall.com

The Village in Wauwatosa
wauwatosavillage.org

Pizzeria Piccola
7606 W State St.
Wauwatosa, WI 53213
pizzeriapiccola.com

BROWSE THE BOOKS
AT BOSWELL

For decades, the Harry W. Schwartz Bookshop was the iconic independent bookseller for the Milwaukee area. Although that store is now closed, its creative and independent spirit still remains strong at Boswell Book Company, which was founded by Daniel Goldin, the longtime book buyer for Harry W. Schwartz. Boswell is an eclectic and vibrant bookstore known for its passionate and helpful staff and popular author events. It's fun to browse Boswell's wide and intriguing selection not quite knowing what you're looking for. Let the staff (known as the Boswellians) offer a special recommendation, or see what featured author might be in the shop in the near future. On the shelves, you'll find used books in good condition intermingled with the new.

Family friendly

Boswell Book Company
2559 N Downer Ave., Milwaukee, WI 53211
boswell.indiebound.com

SUGGESTED ITINERARIES

BEER AND BREWING

Take a Brewery Tour, 2
Raise a Glass in a Beer Garden, 13
Explore Extensive Beer Lists in Bay View, 26
Go on a Pedaling Pub Crawl, 75
See How the Beer Barons Lived, 90
Pay Your Respects to Milwaukee's Late Greats, 95
Take Home Some Beer Memorabilia, 118

THE GREAT OUTDOORS

Raise a Glass in a Beer Garden, 13
Relax on Milwaukee's Best Patio, 28
Kayak through the City, 62
Explore the Oak Leaf Trail, 64
Play Beach Volleyball on Bradford Beach, 66
Go Sailing on Lake Michigan, 68
Explore Milwaukee's Free Outdoor Art Gallery, 69
Explore the City on Two Wheels, 71
Relax on a River Cruise, 74
Go on a Pedaling Pub Crawl, 75
Go Fly a Kite, 76

Check out a 24-Hour Bike Race, 77

Go Ice Skating Downtown, 79

Cheer on Rowing Teams on the Milwaukee River, 80

Explore the Urban Outdoors, 78

Experience Art in Nature, 91

Explore the Original Soldiers Home, 99

Find Milwaukee Murals, 107

DATE NIGHT

Sip a Drink at Milwaukee's Oldest Cocktail Lounge, 6

Take a Food Tour, 18

Cooking Class (or Dinner) at Braise, 20

Get Tropical at Tiki Bars, 25

A Night at the Theater, 48

See a Show at the Pabst Theater, 38

Celebrate Art on Gallery Night, 93

ARTS AND THEATER

See a Movie at the Oriental Theatre, 43

A Night at the Theater, 48

See Broadway in Milwaukee, 49

Enjoy Sweet Strings at the Symphony, 58

Bask in the Ballet, 59

Explore Milwaukee's Free Outdoor Art Gallery, 69
Visit the World's Sexiest Building, 86
Celebrate Art on Gallery Night, 93
Experience Art in Nature, 91
Get to Work at the Grohmann, 104
Find Arts and Style in the Historic Third Ward, 69

FAMILY FUN

Try the Flavor of the Day at Kopp's Frozen Custard, 4
Complete a Mission at the Safe House, 8
Celebrate at Ethnic Festivals, 39
Jam at Summer Concerts, 40
Take Your Picture with the Bronze Fonz, 42
Eat a Cream Puff at the Fair, 44
Walk on the Wild Side, 46
Learn about an American Icon, 47
Crack up at the Longest Running Comedy Show, 52
Let Kids Explore a Pint-Sized Community, 53
Introduce the Kids to Theater, 55
Vive la France!, 56
Watch the Jets at the Air Show, 57
Catch a Game at Miller Park, 63
Go Fly a Kite, 76
Meet the Raptors, 83
Visit the World's Sexiest Building, 86
Discover Discovery World, 88

Visit the Streets of Old Milwaukee, 89

Find What You Didn't Know You Were Looking For, 120

GIRLS WEEKEND

Sip a Drink at Milwaukee's Oldest Cocktail Lounge, 6

Grab Lunch at the Milwaukee Public Market, 11

Tea at the Pfister, 19

Sample Small Plates, 22

Get Lucky at the Casino, 51

Hit the Dance Floor at Mad Planet, 54

Kayak through the City, 62

Root for Roller Derby, 70

Relax on a River Cruise, 74

Go on a Pedaling Pub Crawl, 75

Celebrate Art on Gallery Night, 93

Find Arts and Style in the Historic Third Ward, 110

Stroll through Charming Cedarburg, 113

Shop Local at Sparrow Collective, 116

Wander in Wauwatosa, 122

LOCAL EATS

Try the Flavor of the Day at Kopp's Frozen Custard, 4

Dig into Friday Fish Fry, 5

Try a Giant Pretzel, 10

Grab Lunch at the Milwaukee Public Market, 11

Munch on Some Cheese Curds, 12

Sip an Extreme Bloody Mary, 24

Sample the Freshest Cheese in the City, 30

Eat a Cream Puff at the State Fair, 44

UNIQUE NIGHTLIFE

Sip a Drink at Milwaukee's Oldest Cocktail Lounge, 6

Complete a Mission at the Safe House, 8

Sip an Extreme Bloody Mary, 24

Explore Extensive Beer Lists in Bay View, 26

Get Tropical at Tiki Bars, 25

Geek out at 42 Lounge, 32

Close Wolski's, 33

Play Some Ping-Pong, 34

Bowl at Holler House, 72

Go on a Pedaling Pub Crawl, 75

EVENTS
BY SEASON

SPRING

Catch a Game at Miller Park, 63

Root for Roller Derby, 70

SUMMER

Raise a Glass in a Beer Garden, 13

Relax on Milwaukee's Best Patio, 28

Rock out at the World's Largest Music Festival, 36

Celebrate at Ethnic Festivals, 39

Jam at Summer Concerts, 40

Eat a Cream Puff at the State Fair, 44

Take in an Outdoor Movie for Grown-Ups, 50

Vive la France!, 56

Watch the Jets at the Air Show, 57

Kayak through the City, 62

Play Beach Volleyball on Bradford Beach, 66

Go Sailing on Lake Michigan, 68

Check out a 24-Hour Bike Race, 77

FALL

A Night at the Theater, 48
See Broadway in Milwaukee, 49
Cheer on the Bucks, 65
Cheer on Rowing Teams on the Milwaukee River, 80
Be a Packer Backer, 81
Watch the Ads Take the Ice, 84

WINTER

Go Ice Skating Downtown, 79
Do the Wave for the Wave, 82

INDEX

42 Lounge, 32

American Science & Surplus, 120

Anodyne Coffee, 14–15

Antiques on Second, 112

Balzac, 23

Barnacle Bud's, 28

Basilica of St. Josaphat, 96

Bastille Days, 56

Best Place at the Pabst Brewery, 118

Betty Brinn Children's Museum, 53

BMO Harris Bradley Center, 65, 84

Boswell Book Company, 124

Bradford Beach, 66

Braise Restaurant, 20

Brass Rooster/The Hen House, 111

Brewcity Bruisers, 70

Broadway Paper, 110

Bronze Fonz, 42

Bryant's Cocktail Lounge, 6

Bublr Bikes, 71

Burnhearts, 27

Cafe Centraal, 27

Camp Bar, 81

Cedar Creek Settlement, 113

Central Library, 102

Central Standard Craft Distillery, 16

Charles Allis Art Museum, 101

Chill on the Hill, 40–41

Clock Shadow Creamery, 30

Colectivo Coffee, 14–15

ComedySportz, 52

Denim Bar MKE, 110

Discovery World, 50, 68, 88

Doors Open, 94

Estabrook Beer Garden, 13

Evolution Gastro Pong, 34

Fish Fry & a Flick, 50

First Stage Children's Theater, 49

Florentine Opera, 49

Forest Home Cemetery, 95

Foundation Tiki Bar, 25

Gallery Night & Day, 93

German Fest, 39

Gift of Wings, 76

Girl in the Moon Brewery Shop, The, 118

Glorioso's Italian Market, 117

Great Lakes Distillery, 16

Green Bay Packers, 81

Grohmann Museum, 104

Growing Power, 106

Harley-Davidson Museum, 47

Henry Maier Festival Park, 36, 39

Historic Milwaukee, 94, 97

Historic Third Ward, 75, 93, 110

Holler House, 72

Hot*Pop, 110

Hover Craft, 119

Irish Fest, 39

Jackson's Blue Ribbon Pub, 12

Jazz in the Park, 12

Jewish Museum Milwaukee, 100–101

Kopp's Frozen Custard, 4

La Merenda, 23

Lakefront Brewery, 2, 5, 103

Lucky Joe's Tiki Room, 25

Lynden Sculpture Garden, 91

Mad Planet, 54

Mader's, 10, 114–115

Major Goolsby's, 81

Maker Market, 119

Marcus Center for the Performing Arts, 49, 55, 58–59

Mayfair Mall, 122–123

Mexican Fiesta, 39

Miller Park, 63, 103

MillerCoors, 2–3, 118

Milwaukee Admirals, 84

Milwaukee Air & Water Show, 57

Milwaukee Art Museum, 86, 97, 103

Milwaukee Ballet, 49, 59

Milwaukee Boat Line, 74

Milwaukee Brewers, 63

Milwaukee Bucks, 65

Milwaukee County Zoo, 46

Milwaukee County Winter Farmers Market, 121

Milwaukee Food & City Tours, 18

Milwaukee Kayak Company, 62

Milwaukee Mural Map, 107

Milwaukee Public Market, 11

Milwaukee Public Museum, 89

Milwaukee Repertory Theater, 48

Milwaukee River Challenge, 80

Milwaukee River Cruise Line, 74

Milwaukee RiverWalk, 80

Milwaukee Symphony Orchestra, 49, 58

Milwaukee Wave, 82

Mitchell Park Horticultural Conservatory (The Domes), 92

Museum of Wisconsin Art, 100–101

North Point, 100

North Point Lighthouse, 100

Oak Leaf Trail, 64

Odd Duck, 23

Old World Third Street, 114

Oriental Theatre, 43

Pabst Mansion, 90

Pabst Theater, 38

Packing House, The, 5

Palm Tavern, 27

Pedal Tavern, 75

Pfister Hotel, 19

Pizzeria Piccola, 122–123

Polish Fest, 39

Potawatomi Hotel & Casino, 51

River Rhythms, 40

Riverwest 24, 77

Romans' Pub, 27

Safe House, 8

Sanford Restaurant, 29

Schlitz Audubon Nature Center, 83

Shaker's Cigar Bar, 21

Slice of Ice, 79

Sobelman's Pub-n-Grill, 24

Soldiers Home, 99

Sparrow Collective, 116

Sprecher Brewing Company, 2–3

St. Joan of Arc Chapel, 98

Stone Creek Coffee, 15

Sugar Maple, 27

Summerfest, 36

S/V *Denis Sullivan*, 68

Untapped Tours, 103

Urban Ecology Center, 78

Usinger's Famous Sausage, 115

UW-Milwaukee Panther Arena, 70, 82

Villa Terrace Decorative Arts Museum, 100–101

Village in Wauwatosa, The, 123

Wauwatosa, 122–123

Wisconsin Cheese Mart, 114–115

Wisconsin State Fair, 44

Wolf Peach, 23

Wolski's Tavern, 33